Personalities and Products

Recent Titles in
Contributions to the Study of Mass Media and Communications

The Best of the Rest: Non-Syndicated Newspaper Columnists Select
Their Best Work
Sam G. Riley, editor

Advertising, Alcohol Consumption, and Abuse: A Worldwide Survey
Joseph C. Fisher

Beyond Agendas: New Directions in Communication Research
Philip Gaunt, editor

The Press and Politics in Israel: *The Jerusalem Post* from 1932 to the
Present
Erwin Frenkel

The Disabled, the Media, and the Information Age
Jack A. Nelson, editor

Censorship of Expression in the 1980s: A Statistical Survey
John B. Harer and Steven R. Harris

The U.S. Media and the Middle East: Image and Perception
Yahya R. Kamalipour

Advertising, Alcohol Consumption, and Mortality: An Empirical
Investigation
Joseph C. Fisher and Peter A. Cook

The Press in Times of Crisis
Lloyd E. Chiasson, Jr.

Native Americans in the News: Images of Indians in the Twentieth
Century Press
Mary Ann Weston

Rights vs. Responsibilities: The Supreme Court and the Media
Elizabeth Blanks Hindman

The Press on Trial: Crimes and Trials as Media Events
Lloyd Chiasson, Jr., editor

Personalities and Products

A HISTORICAL PERSPECTIVE ON ADVERTISING IN AMERICA

Edd Applegate

Contributions to the Study of
Mass Media and Communications, Number 53

GREENWOOD PRESS
Westport, Connecticut • London

Library of Congress Cataloging-in-Publication Data

Applegate, Edd.
    Personalities and products : a historical perspective on
advertising in America / Edd Applegate.
        p.   cm.—(Contributions to the study of mass media and
communications, ISSN 0732–4456 ; no. 53)
    Includes bibliographical references and index.
    ISBN 0–313–30364–9 (alk. paper)
    1. Advertising—United States—History. I. Title. II. Series.
HF5813.U6A67   1998
659.1'0973—dc21   97–26893

British Library Cataloguing in Publication Data is available.

Library of Congress Catalog Card Number: 97–26893
ISBN: 0–313–30364–9
ISSN: 0732–4456

First published in 1998

Greenwood Press, 88 Post Road West, Westport, CT 06881
An imprint of Greenwood Publishing Group, Inc.

Printed in the United States of America

The paper used in this book complies with the
Permanent Paper Standard issued by the National
Information Standards Organization (Z39.48–1984).

10 9 8 7 6 5 4 3 2

This book is for Eva.

Contents

Preface

This book is about certain individuals who, in some instances, not only made considerable fortunes in their lifetimes but contributed greatly to advertising.

In Chapter 1, printers who published newspapers and magazines in the American colonies are discussed. The discussion primarily concerns the differences between the printers, their respective newspapers or magazines, and, of course, the advertisements that they accepted for publication.

Chapter 2 examines the first major advertising agents, specifically Volney B. Palmer, George P. Rowell, and Francis Wayland Ayer, and their contributions to advertising as a profession.

Chapter 3 concerns P. T. Barnum's life and his contributions to advertising and marketing. Part of this chapter was presented in 1993 in different form at the Popular Culture Association's National Convention, which was held in New Orleans.

Chapter 4 discusses Lydia Pinkham, the advertising of her controversial but supposedly effective vegetable compound, and the journalistic campaign against the patent medicine industry by certain muckrakers.

Chapter 5 examines John Wanamaker, who was responsible for one of the largest retail stores of his day. Wanamaker's success was due partly to his ability to create effective advertisements and innovative forms of promotion.

Chapter 6 focuses on Albert Lasker and the Lord and Thomas

Advertising Agency, which he eventually owned, and the contributions he made to the creative and business aspects of advertising. Part of this chapter was presented in 1997 in different form at the American Academy of Advertising's Conference, which was held in St. Louis.

Chapter 7 discusses the first 100 years of Procter & Gamble and the company's efforts to manufacture products that consumers needed as well as the company's efforts to sell the products. Part of the discussion focuses on Harley Procter, who successfully advertised Ivory soap; several advertisements for Ivory soap; and William Cooper Procter, who introduced several revolutionary concepts into the everyday management of the company.

Chapter 8 presents the Springs Cotton Mills' advertising campaign of the late 1940s and early 1950s, which was created by the company's owner and president, Elliott White Springs, and which became controversial because of the advertisements' illustrations of scantily clad young women and the accompanying blocks of copy that contained questionable descriptive terms.

Of course, the purpose of this book is to share some insight into the lives of these individuals as well as some insight into their contributions to advertising. In order to do the latter, numerous advertisements for which these individuals were directly or indirectly responsible have been included and discussed in the hope that readers will understand more fully how the individuals thought.

Acknowledgments

This book would not have been possible without the assistance of certain individuals, libraries, advertising agencies, and corporations.

I am indebted to Betty McFall and other librarians at the Todd Library, Middle Tennessee State University, for their guidance and help in securing specific articles and books.

I wish to thank the staffs at the following for their valuable support: the Learning Center at Messiah College, the St. Louis Public Library, the Nashville Public Library, the Library of Congress, the library at Lutheran Theological Seminary at Gettysburg, the library at the Union Theological Seminary, the library at the University of Mississippi, the library at Eastern Mennonite University, the Historical Society of Pennsylvania, the library at East Tennessee State University, the library at the University of Tennessee at Chattanooga, the library at Austin Peay State University, the library at the University of South Carolina, the library at the University of Oklahoma, the library at the University of Tennessee in Memphis, the library at Tennessee Technological University, the library at Carson-Newman College, the Pius XII Library at Saint Louis University, the Kansas City Public Library, the library at the University of Tennessee at Knoxville, and the Worcester Public Library.

I wish to thank the executives of Procter & Gamble, Cincinnati, Ohio; the executives of Springs Industries, Inc., Fort Mill, South

Carolina; and the executives of the N. W. Ayer & Partners advertising agency, New York, for their kind responses to my inquiries. I wish to thank the director of the P. T. Barnum Museum, Bridgeport, Connecticut, for information about P. T. Barnum.

I wish to thank Marilyn Brownstein, former editor at Greenwood Publishing Group, who helped me with an earlier book. I wish to thank George Butler, editor at Greenwood, who helped me with an earlier book. I wish to thank G. Nick Street and Liz Murphy, editors at Praeger, who helped me with an earlier book. I wish to thank James Ice, my editor at Greenwood, who believed in this book. I also wish to thank the other editors and staff members at Greenwood who were involved in the production of this book.

1

Advertising in Colonial America

INTRODUCTION

Termed the year of the Restoration, primarily because King Charles II returned from his exile of 17 years, 1660 marked the beginning of what was to become a dramatic change in England's history. Between 1660 and 1789, England grew into a neo-classical empire that saw a great influx of immigrants, expeditions to other countries (including America and India), and the rise of Parliament as a powerful force in the English political structure. This neo-classical age, however, came to an end when the Industrial Revolution began.

Although restored to the throne, Charles II was not without critics. Though many believed his reign would be an exceptional one, within years they saw that he was interested in what the French had to offer (since his exile had been in France), not in what his English subjects desired.

Charles II, a Catholic, did, however, resign himself to his ministers' wishes and allow them control of the government. As a result, the Church of England reigned while Puritanism suffered. Oliver Cromwell was dead, along with other Puritan leaders. Until Charles II died in 1685, English society was chaotic to a certain extent. For instance, the King failed to produce an heir to the throne; the bubonic plague killed thousands of English citizens in 1665; the Great Fire of London, which immediately followed, killed hundreds more; a brief war with Holland erupted in the mid-1660s; and an anti-Catholic rebellion occurred in the late 1670s.

When Charles II died, his brother, James II, succeeded him as king and for three years flaunted his Catholicism. The duke of Monmouth, who was Charles II's natural, but illegitimate, son, attempted to overthrow James II and was subsequently executed. Tensions between persons of different religions mounted until the king issued a Declaration of Indulgence that granted citizens of England the freedom of worship. Protestants had believed that the successor to the throne would be Mary, the king's daughter (as well as an Anglican), who had married William of Orange. When they realized that the king's newborn son, a baptized Catholic, might become king, they immediately rebelled. Consequently, James II lost his throne in 1688 to William and Mary.

Although William and Mary were welcomed to the throne, Parliament exercised its power, and William and Mary had to accept a Bill of Rights. No longer did a king or queen have power because of his or her heredity. The power was granted by Parliament, although the two-party system, Tories and Whigs (Cavaliers and Puritans), which appeared during Cromwell's reign, failed to have an impact on English rule until after Mary's death in 1695 and William's death in 1702, when Mary's sister, Anne, became queen. During her reign a bitter struggle for power between the two parties erupted. When Anne died in 1714, the Whigs gained control and drove out the Tories.

The members of Parliament demanded that the next queen or king be a Protestant. George, who became George I, king of the United Kingdom of Great Britain (England and Scotland had united under Anne's reign), was the only Protestant heir. George, who was the son of Sophia of Hanover, Germany, the granddaughter of James I, was not particularly interested in politics. Thus, Parliament had a free hand. When George II succeeded his father to the throne in 1727 he, too, was disenchanted with English government. He was succeeded by his son, George III, in 1760, during the Seven Years' War (1756–1763), in which England successfully acquired Canada from France. George III, although he tried to be a better king than his father and grandfather, failed to realize that England's colonial philosophy, which affected India, Canada, and America, was creating tensions abroad, especially in America. English society suffered from disease probably caused by unsanitary conditions. Personal hygiene was not a high priority. Thieves, especially highwaymen, robbed and murdered English citizens who tried to ride to town. London, of course, was not as it is today. Before thousands of buildings burned in the Great Fire they were, for the most part, unkempt, compared to today. Those who lived in rural areas were mostly backward, since they seldom rode to town to hear the latest gossip. Those who lived in London had to walk or ride on unkempt streets. If they shopped or visited a coffeehouse, they did so during the day; during the night murderers and thieves roamed the streets searching for victims.

As Britain prospered, first, from a large trade in the import and reexport of colonial produce; second, from a large trade in the export of agricultural produce such as grain; and third from the Industrial Revolution, its citizenry became enlightened from frequent visits to coffeehouses rebuilt of stone and from writers who advocated certain reforms. Although problems such as war with another country plagued the empire, the empire survived. Even the internal bickering between Tory and Whig and between Parliament and king could not destroy the nation's people.

The political and social upheaval mentioned earlier actually encouraged writers to present certain perspectives. Richard Steele, for instance, published the *Tatler*, a newspaper that appeared three times a week. Steele and, later, Joseph Addison contributed not only light, entertaining news stories but satiric essays on morals or manners and certain prominent citizens. Occasionally, Steele included an attack on gambling, dueling, brutality, or drinking. Addison, in addition to contributing to Steele's *Tatler*, published the *Spectator*, which was a more polished *Tatler*. Addison wrote entertaining articles and essays. His philosophy about man was voiced by personae, including the popular Sir Roger de Coverly.

In the September 12–September 14, 1710, issue of the *Tatler*, Isaac Bickerstaff (Steele or Addison) discussed the importance of advertising:

But to consider this Subject in its most ridiculous Lights, Advertisements are of great Use to the Vulgar: First of all, as they are Instruments of Ambition. A Man that is by no Means big enough for the *Gazette*, may easily creep into the Advertisements . . .

A Second Use which this Sort of Writings have been turned to of late Years, has been the Management of Controversy, insomuch that above half the Advertisements one meets with now-a-Days are purely Polemical.

The Third and last Use of the Writings is, to inform the World where they may be furnished with almost every Thing that is necessary for Life. If a Man has Pains in his Head, Cholicks in his Bowels, or Spots in his Clothes, he may here meet with proper Cures and Remedies. If a Man would recover a Wife or a Horse that is stolen or strayed; if he wants new Sermons, Electuaries, Asses Milk, or any Thing else, either for his Body or his Mind, this is the Place to look for them in.[1]

The same issue of the *Tatler* illustrated Bickerstaff's favorable position toward advertising; numerous copy-filled advertisements appeared under the heading "Advertisements." The *Tatler* was like other newspapers published in England in the sense that advertisements were encouraged.

Under Charles II, England furthered its expansion in America. It occupied the Atlantic coast from Canada to Florida. Pennsylvania was founded, and Philadelphia, which had been founded in 1682, became the greatest river port in America. Carolina was founded, and plantations, which were farmed by slaves, were developed. The chartered colonies became Crown colonies, and governors appointed by the Crown replaced proprietors or managers. The influx of Puritans and Cavaliers increased the colonies' population, and the Indians were eventually stripped of their land.

Boston, Newport, New York, Philadelphia, and Charleston became not only the dominant colonial settlements but marketing centers. Specific days of the week became "market days." Designated marketplaces were established on the village squares for trading activities. As a result, these five colonies controlled the economy, and each colony regulated wholesale and retail trade.[2]

Large quantities of southern commodities could be processed and exported. Production in the North was on a smaller scale but more diversified. What was produced could be distributed to the various markets in America.[3]

Before 1700 retailing consisted of small shops owned by craftsmen who made and sold certain goods and small stores operated by colonists who would buy goods for resale. Between 1690 and 1720, in Boston, Newport, New York, Philadelphia, and Charleston, specialty shops emerged primarily because of increased urbanization and a higher standard of living. At this time, the so-called Yankee peddler roamed the country, competing against the more established merchants.[4]

Eventually, the older, more established merchants attempted to have legislation enacted that would protect their businesses. They also desired regulations that covered standards, weights, and selling practices. The Yankee peddler was an enemy to the merchant because he went to the customer and used theatrics to sell his wares. Enacted legislation was restrictive, but it actually decreased the abuse in trade practices, which was positive. The economy developed, and new marketing institutions emerged. Retailing continued to grow, and dry goods or general stores appeared on the landscape.[5]

Other colonies such as Georgia were founded. However, the colonists were hemmed in by the French and Indians, and England, although it was the mother country, failed to help the colonists in their struggle to survive. Instead, laws were enacted to prohibit colonists from selling anything other than agricultural goods to England. Concurrently, whenever something was purchased, it had to come from England. Tariffs were placed on certain imports to keep the colonists from buying those products, and laws were passed to limit what could be produced, such as iron. On the other hand, the navigation acts strengthened the shipping industry of the northern colonies.

To the colonists one king or queen was as evil as the next; it made little difference whether James II, William and Mary, Anne, George I, George II, or George III reigned. The colonists' problems remained the same. Yet, they had to be happy when England won the Seven Years' War, for it captured for the British Empire what had belonged to France: Canada. Subsequently, the fear of being invaded by France was eliminated.

Various social and economic groups used and accepted credit

as a substitute for exchange primarily because coins were scarce. Credit had a stimulating effect on the welfare of the colonists because it allowed not only production but consumption on a scale that would otherwise have been impossible. However, as Benjamin Franklin and others pointed out, there were abuses.[6]

When the Crown and Parliament began to restrict American expansion as well as limit American trade, the colonists grew angry. When various acts were imposed, colonists realized that Britain was trying to tax them for revenue. Although repeated demonstrations forced Parliament to repeal certain acts, other measures were enacted to serve the same function as the acts. Eventually, certain writers convinced the colonists to unite and boycott British goods. In 1770 certain measures were repealed. Three years later the Tea Act, which fostered the Boston Tea Party of the same year, and subsequently the "Intolerable Acts" forced the citizens of Massachusetts to arm themselves for combat. Delegates from 12 colonies attended the First Continental Congress at Philadelphia in 1774 and pledged to defend Massachusetts. The Congress also made demands on Britain that Britain would not meet. When Governor Thomas Gage, who was also commander in chief of the British army in America, was ordered to reestablish British rule, his military action initiated the War of Independence, a war that began in 1775 and ended in 1783.

America won its independence, and each colony became a state. But the central government faced many problems, including the ratification of the Constitution.

American society was basically rural and poor. Puritans as well as other colonists lived on farms; few lived in cities, although cities grew rapidly because of the influx of people from other countries. If the farmer or plantation owner visited a city, he would have to travel on roads made of mud; if he made his destination without loss of pocketbook or limb, he would find streets made of cobblestones or gravel or, in some cases, dirt. But this was merely the beginning of an experience he would not forget.

According to John M. Blum et al.:

The farmer had been told that the city was a nursery of vice and prodigality. He now saw that it was so. Every shop had wares to catch his eye: exquisite fabrics, delicate chinaware, silver buckles, looking glasses, and other imported luxuries that never reached the crossroads store. Putting up at the tavern, he found himself drinking too much rum. And there were willing girls, he heard, who had lost their virtue and would be glad to help him lose his. Usually he returned to the farm to warn his children as he had been warned. He seldom understood that the vice of the city, if not its prodigality, was mainly for transients like himself. Permanent residents had work to do.[7]

Those who lived in cities were merchants who purchased or traded produce, shipwrights who constructed ships, millers, instrument makers, coopers, schoolmasters, barbers, craftsmen, and a host of others. However, those who lived in cities faced problems such as crime, filth, fires, and poverty that others did not. Many of the jobs in cities depended on overseas trade. Thus, if trade was bad, jobs disappeared, and, according to Blum et al., "the men and women who lived by them had no place to turn. As cities grew, so did the numbers of the poor and unemployed who had to be cared for."[8]

In order to tame a harsh wilderness, work had to be done, and the Puritans, among others, performed remarkably well. Though they feared God, they enjoyed the vices of man, including drink and occasionally adulterous sex. Still, the religious views of John Calvin dominated their lives. Predestination instilled in them a spark that ultimately ignited their will to achieve what men had not achieved before: freedom to grow strong both spiritually and economically.

Although witch-hunts occurred in the 1690s, and differences between Puritan, Anglican, and Quaker philosophies stirred fanatics to commit physical atrocities such as imprisonment or banishment before the 1700s, after 1720 religion experienced the "Great Awakening." Revivals, which were more emotional than intellectual, were held throughout the colonies for society's lower classes. From the Dutch Reformed churches of New Jersey to the Scotch-Irish Presbyterian churches of Pennsylvania, revivalism, because it made religion more personal, prospered throughout the 1700s.

In his autobiography, Benjamin Franklin discussed Reverend Whitefield, who had arrived from Ireland. Reverend Whitefield journeyed throughout the colonies, preaching to various congregations. Although Franklin was not easily manipulated, he explained what happened to him when he attended one of Reverend Whitefield's sermons:

I happened soon after to attend one of his Sermons, in the Course of which I perceived he intended to finish with a Collection, and I silently resolved he should get nothing from me. I had in my Pocket a Handful of Copper, Money, three or four silver Dollars, and five Pistoles in Gold. As he proceeded I began to soften, and concluded to give the Coppers. Another Stroke of his Oratory made me asham'd of that, and determin'd me to give the Silver; and he finish'd so admirably, that I empty'd my Pocket wholly into the Collector's Dish, Gold and all.[9]

Many colonists were affected by these preachers.

During this period, social, educational, and political institutions were founded. Colleges prepared students for the ministry and enlightened them in physics, philosophy, and psychology. Literature, too, appeared. From histories and autobiographies, to plays and novels, colonists were provided entertainment. Perhaps the most important form of entertainment was the newspaper, which was not only read but discussed at the local tavern or coffeehouse.

COLONIAL NEWSPAPER ADVERTISING

The first printing presses in America arrived in the 1600s. Prior to this time advertising appeared in pamphlet and, later, signboard forms. Neither form appeared, however, until settlements had populations to warrant each form's use.

Pamphlets, which were popular, explained in depth what was available. Signboards, on the other hand, resembled in design those used in England. Most of the time these signs contained symbols as well as addresses, but not numbers. For example, various symbols were used for tobacco shops—from the black boy and the Indian to the Smoking Dutchman. Addresses consisted of brief copy. Although these signs were popular among businesses throughout the colonies, the most colorful appeared in cities such as Philadelphia and Baltimore. Signs for taverns were the most visible.

The printing press had been in the colonies for more than 50 years before it was used to print a newspaper. Boston had several presses, while Philadelphia and New York had at least one each. These presses printed the Bible, the *Freeman's Oath*, almanacs, and other books. One press in Boston was used to print tracts. Contrary to popular belief, most authorities in the colonies prohibited operators of printing presses from printing newspapers. In certain colonies, like Boston, even religious literature was restricted.

On September 25, 1690, the first newspaper appeared in Boston. Titled *Publick Occurrences, Both Forreign and Domestick*, it was published by Benjamin Harris and printed by R. Pierce. The newspaper differed from its broadside predecessors in the sense that it focused on American, not European, news.

Charles E. Clark wrote, "Harris intended primarily to save Bostonians during an exceptionally critical time from rumors and 'False Reports' of the events and affairs, especially the martial affairs, of their own province."[10]

Although the authorities declared that the paper was a "pamphlet," they prohibited Harris from publishing another issue. Had it not been for the authorities, the newspaper in the New World would have succeeded sooner, and advertising would have found a new medium. Unfortunately, Harris did not have time to improve his newspaper by adding advertising.

In the early 1700s, John Campbell, who was postmaster in Boston, knew several important politicians, including Governor Fitz John Winthrop of Connecticut. Campbell, using his position and his friends, eventually asked the authorities to grant him permission to publish a newspaper. He was granted permission. The *Boston News-Letter*, which was dated "From Monday April 17 to Monday April 24, 1704," contained the following information:

Advertisement

This News-Letter is to be continued Weekly; and all Persons who have any Houses, Lands, Tenements, Farms, Ships, Vessels, Goods, Wares or Merchandizes, &c. to be Sold, or Let; or Servants Run-away, or Goods Stole or Lost; may have the same inserted at a Reasonable Rate, from

Twelve Pence to *Five Shillings*, and not to exceed: Who may agree with *John Campbell* Post-master of *Boston*.

All Persons in Town and Country may have said News-Letter every Week, Yearly, upon reasonable terms, agreeing with *John Campbell*, Postmaster for the same.[11]

The *News-Letter* was printed on an 8" × 12" sheet of paper. Copy appeared in two columns on the front and back. Rough in appearance, the *News-Letter* contained news from newspapers published in London. Often the news was out-of-date. The advertising, which was limited by the publisher, received a maximum space of 20 lines. The cost per agate line was about 1½ cents.

The third *News-Letter*, dated May 1–8, 1704, contained the first paid advertisements. Although there were three advertisements, together they occupied only four inches of space in one column. The only headline that separated them from the news was the word "advertisements." Two advertised rewards for the capture of thieves; one advertisement read:

Lost on 10th of April last off Mr. Shippen's Wharf in Boston, Two Iron Anvils, weighing between 120–140 pounds each; Whoever has taken them up, and will bring or give true intelligence of them to John Campbell, Postmaster, shall have a sufficient reward.[12]

The third advertised real estate—the first real estate advertisement to appear in an American newspaper:

At Oysterbay, on *Long Island* in the Province of *N. York*, There is a very good Fulling-Mill, to be Let or Sold, as also a Plantation, having on it a large new Brick house, and another good house by it for a Kitchen & work house, with a Barn, Stable &c. a young Orchard, and 20 acres clear Land. The Mill is to be Let with or without the Plantation: Enquire of Mr. *William Bradford* Printer in *N. York*, and know further.[13]

As Campbell's *News-Letter* continued, other kinds of advertising appeared. In the May 15–22, 1704, issue, an advertisement targeted men who desired to sail:

CAPTAIN Peter Lawrence is going a Privateering from Rhode Island in a good Sloop, about 60 Tons, six Guns, and 90 men for Canada, and any Gentlemen or Sailors that are disposed to go shall be kindly entertained.[14]

Advertisements for slaves appeared frequently, as the following example illustrates:

A NEGRO Woman about 16 years Old, to be sold by John Campbell, Postmaster, to be seen at his House, next door to the Anchor Tavern.[15]

The first advertisement for a store appeared in the August 21, 1704, issue:

AT Mr. *John Miro* Merchant, his Warehouse upon the Dock in Boston, There is to be Sold good Cordage of all sizes, from a Spurn-yarn to Cables of 13 inches, by whole-sail or Retail.[16]

Advertising was restricted in the *Boston News-Letter*; even after three years five inches devoted to advertising was rare. Some issues were devoid of any advertising whatsoever.

However, as trade and commerce expanded in the colonies, the *Boston News-Letter's* circulation increased. As a result, the publishers enlarged the paper's size—from two pages to four. They also accepted more advertisements. As Sidney Kobre wrote:

By 1750, a column of advertising appeared regularly, two columns frequently. Occasionally, three columns of advertisements were published. The *News-Letter* had become a more stable business enterprise by the mid-century. It had advanced far from the puny sheet with two pages which Campbell first issued in 1704.[17]

On December 21, 1719, in Boston, William Brooker published the *Boston Gazette*. This paper became the postmaster's organ when Brooker was appointed postmaster. The next day, in Philadelphia, Andrew Bradford published the *American Weekly Mercury*. Both newspapers were similar to the *News-Letter* in size and typography. Even the advertisements were similar, except that

Brooker employed brief headlines that actually identified what the various advertisements concerned.

Two years later, James Franklin, Benjamin's older brother, published the *New England Courant* in Boston. When he published controversial political essays, he was sent to jail. Benjamin, who was just 16, became editor of the *Courant*. Benjamin Franklin wrote,

During my Brother's Confinement, which I resented a good deal, notwithstanding our private Differences, I had the Management of the Paper, and I made bold to give our Rulers some Rubs in it, which my Brother took very kindly, while others began to consider me in an unfavourable Light, as a young Genius that had a Turn for Libelling & Satyr.[18]

Franklin printed the word "advertisements" in bold capital letters and separated it from the copy. The word undoubtedly attracted attention. Franklin's editorship ended two years later, and he moved to Philadelphia. He worked for Samuel Keimer, who operated a printing shop. Keimer eventually published the *Universal Instructor in All the Arts and Sciences and Pennsylvania Gazette*. Within a few months, Franklin, with the help of H. Meredith, purchased the paper. Immediately, he shortened the name to *Pennsylvania Gazette* and improved the writing and typography. Within several months the *Gazette* was considered by most as the most attractive newspaper in the colonies.

Advertising in the *Gazette* was important to Franklin. In the September 25–October 2, 1729, issue, he printed the word "Advertisements" in bold letters, then left about a half inch of white space. The issue contained nine advertisements. The first letter of the first word of each advertisement was capitalized. In addition, each advertisement had at least one-half inch of white space above and below it. One of the advertisements was for soap:

To be Sold by *Edward Shippen*, choice Hard Soap, very Reasonable.[19]

In the same issue, Franklin advertised that he printed the following:

BIBLES, Testaments, Psalters, Psalm-Books, Accompt-Books, Bills of Lading Bound and unbound, Common Blank Bonds for Money, Bonds with Judgment, Counterbonds, Arbitration Bonds, Arbitration Bonds with Umpirage, Bail Bonds, Counterbonds to save Bail harmless, Bills of Sale, Powers of Attorney, Writs, Summons, Apprentices Indentures, Servants Indentures, Penal Bills, Promisory Notes, &c, all the Blanks in the most authentick Forms, and correctly printed; may be had at the Publishers of this Paper; who perform all other Sorts of Printing at reasonable Rates.[20]

Franklin increased the number of pages from two to four so he could handle more advertisements and news stories. He separated each advertisement with white space. He used at least a 14-point heading for each advertisement. Later, he incorporated small stock cuts or illustrations. In the May 23–30, 1734, issue, for instance, he employed a stock cut of a ship for the *Three Batchelors*, which had docked. The advertisement informed merchants that the ship was accepting freight. Franklin realized that illustrations could enhance an advertisement, so he used half-column and column cuts made especially for certain advertisers. Readers could determine for whom or what the advertisement was merely by the illustration. For instance, a cut of a clock face was used to identify a watchmaker's advertisement. Retailers who normally stayed away from advertising in newspapers realized they could increase sales by advertising in Franklin's newspaper. As a result, Franklin had to enlarge his newspaper again. Instead of two short columns, he put in three deep columns, which made the newspaper about the size of a modern tabloid.

In the *Pennsylvania Gazette*'s August 14–21, 1735, issue, Franklin advertised the following product, which he sold:

VERY good COFFEE Sold by the Printer hereof.[21]

Franklin, like other printers of newspapers, published advertisements for slaves. In the June 23–30, 1737, issue, for instance, the following advertisement appeared. The advertisement attracted attention not because of what was being sold but because Franklin italicized most of the copy:

A Fine young Negro Fellow Speaks English, us'd to Labour, and is fit for either Town or Country, to be Sold by James Efdaile *at Mr.* Dering's *in* Front-Street, *or at his Store on* Carpenter's *Wharff, where is also to be sold, good* St. Kitts *Mellasses, Ginger & Indigo.*[22]

In the same issue, Franklin advertised that his wife's prayer book had been stolen from the church. The advertisement is typical in the sense that almost every printer who published a newspaper included advertisements about personal items lost or stolen:

TAKEN out of a Pew in the Church some Months since, a Common Prayer Book, bound in Red, gilt, and letter'd DF on each Corner. The Person who took it, is desir'd to open it and read the *Eighth* Commandment, and afterwards return it into the same Pew again; upon which no further Notice will be taken.[23]

In the same issue, Franklin advertised that he was selling a black woman:

TO BE SOLD

A LIKELY young breeding Negroe Woman, speaks good English, understands her Needle and any sort of Household Work, and has had the Small-Pox. Enquire of the Printer.[24]

In the January 18–25, 1738–1739, issue, Franklin advertised *Poor Richard's Almanac*, which he wrote and published:

Just Published,

POOR RICHARD's ALMANACKS, for the Year 1739. Wherein is contained the Lunations, Eclipses, Judgments of the Weather, Spring-Tides, Planets Motions, and mutual Aspects, Sun and Moon's Rising and Setting, Length of Days, Time of High Water, Fairs, Courts and observable Days. Together with many witty Hints, Sayings, Verses, and Observations, as usual, viz. The Art of Foretelling the Weather. Why he continues to call himself *Poor Richard*. Teague's Criticism on the First of *Genesis*. Giles Jolt's Syllogism. John's Wife. Kings and Bears. Miss Cloe's Cafe. Squire Edward's Kindness. The Knave in Grain. Codrus and Caesar. Bright Florella. The ninth Beatitude. On his late Deafness. An infallible Cure for the Toothach. George's fine Fruitbearing Tree. Lower

County Teeth. The Emblem of a Friend. Modern Faith, Pinchall's Temperance, A——'s Wit. Life a Journey. Homer's Fate. Sam's Lawsuit, &c, &c, &c.

To which is added.

A most true and unerring PROGNOSTICATION for the Year 1739, relating to the Condition of these Northern Colonies, The Diseases the People will be subject to, and the Quantity of the Fruits of the Earth. Sold by *B. Franklin*, Price 3 s. 6 d. per Dozen.[25]

It should be mentioned that Franklin was not the only printer who published an almanac. Several printers who published newspapers also published almanacs.

In the February 15–22, 1738–1739 issue, the following advertisement, which was typical of small merchants, appeared:

TO BE SOLD

By PETER DELAGE, *over-against* Mr. James Steele's, *in* Second-Street, Philadelphia:

CHOICE *Double-and Single-refin'd Loaf-Sugar, Mufcovado Sugar fit for Shop or Family Use, Sugar-Candy, Mollasses, Bohea and Imperial TEAS, all at the cheapest Rates.*[26]

In the June 17, 1742, issue, another small merchant advertised the following:

Lately imported from London, And to be SOLD by Joseph Saunders, At his House next Joe Goodson's, in Chesnut-Street, Philadelphia, the following GOODS, viz.

FINE London Shalloons, Horse Hair and fine mohair Buttons, silk and hair Twist, fine Durettees, sewing Silk and Threads, figured Dimities and Fuftians, Mens and Womens worsted and thread Hose, shammery and sundry other sorts of Gloves, Hat Linings, scotch Handkerchiefs, Womens Clogs and Childrens Shoes, sundry sorts of Shoemaker's Tools, cutlery and hard Ware, Weston's Snuff, fine writing Paper, with sundry other Goods. Also good West-India RUM.[27]

Franklin's newspaper contained advertisements about numerous products and services, including glasses, wine, cheese, chocolate, mathematical instruments, codfish, tea, coffee, and stoves.

No other printer of that time did more for advertising. Without question, advertising in America owes a great debt to Franklin.[28]

In addition to publishing a newspaper and selling various products, including books, Franklin trained others, such as Thomas Whitemarsh, in his printing shop, then sent these individuals into various colonies to establish newspapers. Whitemarsh, for instance, went to South Carolina and established the *South Carolina Gazette* in 1732. Franklin provided financial assistance to these printers and, in turn, received part of the printers' profits.

In his advice to younger Americans who desired to become successful, Franklin wrote:

Remember that Money is of a prolific generating Nature. Money can beget Money, and its Offspring can beget more, and so on. Five Shillings turn'd, is *Six*: Turn'd again, 'tis Seven and Three Pence; and so on 'til it becomes an Hundred Pound. The more there is of it, the more it produces every Turning, so that the Profits rise quicker and quicker. He that kills a breeding Sow, destroys all her Offspring to the thousandth Generation. He that murders a Crown, destroys all it might have produc'd, even Scores of Pounds.[29]

This excerpt exemplified Franklin's philosophy toward business and money. Like other successful entrepreneurs of his day, Franklin was richly rewarded for his untiring labors.

Other printers in the colonies published newspapers. One was William Bradford of New York. In 1725, he published the *New York Gazette*.

In the October 3–10, 1737, issue, Bradford published the following advertisement, which concerned a stay maker who had arrived from London:

Moses Slaughter, Stay-Maker, from *London*, has brought with him a Parcel of extraordinary good and Fashionable Stays, of his own making, of several Sizes and Prices. The Work of them he will warrant to be good, and for Shape, inferiour to none that are made.

He lodges at present at the House of *William Bradford*, next Door but one to the Treasurer's, near the Fly-Market, where he is ready to suit those that want, with extraordinary good Stays. Or he is ready to wait

upon any Ladys or Gentlewomen that please to send for him to their Houses.
If any desire to be informed of the Work he has done, let them enquire of Mrs. *Elliston* in the *Broad-Street*, or of Mrs. *Nichols* in the *broadway*, who have had of his Work.[30]

Whether or not Moses Slaughter paid for the advertisement is unknown. Whether he paid for his room at William Bradford's residence or whether he was Bradford's indentured servant is also unknown.

Bradford also published advertisements for wine, tea, nails, steel, and a host of other products. For instance, in the September 26–October 3, 1737, issue, the following advertisement appeared:

Choice Good Canary Wine to be Sold at *Three Shillings and six Pence per Gallon*, by the Five Gallons, at the Widow *Desbrosses* in Hannover-Square.[31]

Bradford, like Franklin and other printers, sold various products, including almanacs, as the following advertisement illustrates:

TITAN LEED's Almanacks, and W. BIRKET's Almanacks for the year 1738, are now Printed & Sold by *W. Bradford*.[32]

A competitor, John Peter Zenger, published the first issue of the *New York Weekly Journal* on November 5, 1733. Zenger, who published criticism of the provincial government, was arrested for libel. A trial by jury was scheduled, and contrary to the authorities Zenger was found innocent. His lawyer, Andrew Hamilton, orchestrated a masterful defense, and Zenger's verdict triggered what Governor Morris said was "the dawn of that liberty which afterwards revolutionized America."[33]

Zenger's newspaper was superior to Bradford's. The *Journal* contained 8 to 10 advertisements, while the *Gazette* contained two. In addition, Zenger used column rules to separate advertisements, and he did not restrict advertising to a particular amount of space. One advertisement, for instance, was more than a half-page deep. Like Franklin, Zenger realized the importance of illustrations and used various cuts to improve the appearance of certain advertisements.

In the March 29, 1736, issue, Zenger published an advertisement about a cosmetic:

> At Mrs. Edwards next door to Mr. Jamison, opposite the Fort Garden, an admirable Beautifying Wash for Hands, Face and Neck, it makes the Skin soft, smooth and plump, it likewise takes away Redness, Freckles, Sun-Burning, or Pimples, and cures Postules, Itchings, Ring Worms, Tetters, Scurf, Morphew and other like Deformities of the Face and Skin (Intirely free from any Corroding Quality) and brings out an exquisite Beauty, with lip Salve and Tooth Powder, all sold very cheap.[34]

Zenger charged three shillings for the first insertion of an advertisement and one shilling for each insertion thereafter. Although a few printers such as Zenger published rates for advertisements, most did not, because they engaged in bartering. Often individuals could not afford to pay for the advertisements they placed with printers; thus, they bartered with products and/or services.

One of the most innovative newspapers in the mid-1700s was the *New York Post Boy*, which was founded by James Parker in 1742. Parker, who had apprenticed in Franklin's print shop, received financial support from Franklin. Originally titled the *New York Gazette, Revived in the Weekly Post Boy*, and later to *Parker's New York Gazette* or the *Weekly Post Boy*, the newspaper lived until 1773.

Advertisements in Parker's paper occupied as many as six columns, or half of the paper. Advertisements were for real estate, slaves, runaway apprentices, books, wines, medicines, and lotteries. Headlines were capitalized in 10-point, sometimes 14- or 18-point.

By 1760, type sizes and typefaces varied within most advertisements. Headlines were at least 18-point. Display advertisements filled the columns. The newspaper became so successful among advertisers that advertisements filled three of the four pages. The October 30, 1760, issue's front page contained 15 advertisements in its three columns. Franklin's paper had come

Table 1.1
Newspapers Published in the Colonies in 1775

Number	Colony	Towns/Cities — Number
9	Pennsylvania	Philadelphia — 7 (6 in English, 1 in German); Germantown — 1 (in German); Lancaster — 1 (in English and German)
7	Massachusetts	Boston — 5; Salem — 1; Newburyport — 1
4	Connecticut	New London — 1; New Haven — 1; Hartford — 1; Norwich — 1
4	New York	New York — 3; Albany — 1
3	South Carolina	Charleston — 3
2	Maryland	Annapolis — 1; Baltimore — 1
2	North Carolina	Wilmington — 1; Newbern — 1
2	Rhode Island	Newport — 1; Providence — 1
2	Virginia	Williamsburg — 2
1	Georgia	Savannah — 1
1	New Hampshire	Portsmouth — 1

close, but Parker's paper was probably the first in the American colonies to devote the entire front page to advertising.

In 1765, primarily because there was a shortage of paper in the colonies, display advertising was cut from Benjamin Franklin's *Gazette*. Instead of large type and illustrations, small type and thumbnail-size art filled the advertising columns.

According to Isaiah Thomas, there were 37 newspapers in America when the Revolutionary War began in 1775.[35] (See Table 1.1.)

William A. Dill, on the other hand, claimed that there were 48 newspapers being published in 1775.[36] (See Table 1.2.)

It doesn't matter whether Thomas or Dill is correct. What matters is that both indicated that the number of printers, like the population, increased. The number of advertisements appearing in newspapers also increased. Indeed, advertisements filled more than a page in certain newspapers before 1775.

When the Revolutionary War started, conditions worsened, and many newspapers died by the time the war ended. However, one newspaper, the *Pennsylvania Packet and the General Ad-*

Table 1.2
Population, Newspaper, and Circulation Growth (1704–1775)

Year	Population	Number of Newspapers	Number of Subscribers
1704	300,000	1	300
1710	357,500	1	–
1720	500,000	3	3,269
1725	1,000,000	5	–
1730	–	8	–
1740	–	12	–
1750	1,207,000	14	–
1760	1,610,000	21	–
1770	2,205,000	29	–
1775	2,803,000	48	23,300

vertiser, founded in 1771 by John Dunlap, illustrated how advertising could help sell newspapers. It is obvious that Dunlap learned from Franklin. He realized the importance of how an advertisement looked. As a result, the advertisements in his paper were easier to read and attracted reader interest. Dunlap's newspaper featured commercial news, too, rather than political stories. Commercial news attracted merchants. Thus, he was able to attract those who needed to advertise. He revived the illustration, and special cuts were created for certain advertisers. Of course, that the word "advertiser" was part of the newspaper's name helped. Within two years, Dunlap's newspaper was so successful that he had to enlarge its size and increase its columns. At the time, advertising accounted for two-thirds of the paper's content. In 1784, the newspaper, which had started as a weekly, became the first daily to be published in America. The reason was not readers' hunger for news; rather, it was the amount of advertising Dunlap received.

Another daily appeared a year later. Published in New York by Francis Childs, the *New York Daily Advertiser* contributed to advertising by running headlines as big as 36 points. These headlines, usually one word, were printed in bold to capture attention.

According to Sidney Kobre:

The press . . . helped to promote the commerce and prosperity of the new Americans. Through its news columns, its lists of ships clearing and entering, its notes about the West Indies, the colonial newspaper acquainted merchants, shippers and others with facts and information pertinent and valuable to their business.[37]

Kobre noted that colonial printers of newspapers catered to the merchants, farmers, shippers, and fishermen because they depended on them for advertising and subscriptions. Kobre wrote that "the colonial newspaper kept pace with the prosperity of these groups."[38]

Certain publishers in the late 1700s filled the front pages of their newspapers with advertisements in an attempt to attract merchants.

According to Ronald Hoffman, "[T]he merchant employed the newspaper as a retailing agent. Advertising was needed by certain merchants because it served as a means of communication between the seller and the buyer."[39]

Other publishers included advertising supplements in which advertisements filled separate sections. Also, numerous publishers accepted countless advertisements of lotteries. In most instances, these lotteries were conducted to raise money to improve towns or cities. Other lotteries benefited college libraries or churches.[40]

Although most newspapers at this time depended on advertising revenue and street sales, some newspapers were privately supported by political figures for the purpose of spreading political propaganda.

By 1800, the number of newspapers published in the United States was about 300. Most publishers were satisfied with their advertising. Few actually worried about how advertisements appeared. Thus, advertising remained constant in appearance for numerous years. In most cases, no more than one cut illustrated each advertisement. The copy was dull and usually small in size. The reason advertising remained popular among businesses is simple: populations of cities increased. Consequently, proprietors realized that prospective customers were moving close to their enterprises every day; thus, they had to be informed.

The early newspaper advertisements reflected early American

culture. Painters of portraits and houses advertised their services in practically every newspaper that was published along the Atlantic coast. Booksellers, too, advertised, especially those in Boston, which had more booksellers than any other city at the time. Entertaining shows and unusual artists traveled from one colony to another and advertised in various newspapers. Artisans and craftsmen advertised their wares, including various pieces of furniture such as the "Hadley" chest and the popular "Windsor" chair, which they carved. Theaters, the first of which had been built before 1720, became somewhat popular before 1750, and colonists enjoyed watching plays and other forms of theatrical entertainment. Such, of course, was advertised in newspapers.[41]

As James Playsted Wood wrote:

Colonial newspaper advertising was informed by briskness and vitality. It spoke not only of the busyness of small enterprise, the practical considerations of merchants and the purveyors of services, but also of the feelings, beliefs, and prejudices of people in New England and the Middle Colonies. The devious ways of free publicity had not yet been perfected. Men announced their attitudes and opinions in paid advertising. Public relations had not yet taught the importance of moving softly. These advertisers said what they meant and meant what they said.[42]

COLONIAL MAGAZINE ADVERTISING

Magazines lived briefly in the 1700s. Numerous advertisers refused to place advertisements with this medium. No merchant wished to advertise in a magazine that had financial problems, and most magazines had financial problems because advertisers had this attitude. Or, if a printer did not solicit advertisements for a magazine, he soon suffered financially because of his various expenses.

Benjamin Franklin was one of the first printers to plan a magazine for the colonies. However, three days before *The General Magazine, and Historical Chronicle, for All the British Plantations in America* was printed in February 1741, Franklin's rival, Andrew Bradford, printed *The American Magazine, or a Monthly View of the Political State of the British Colonies*. Bradford had learned about Franklin's concept for a magazine from John Webbe. Although Franklin had offered the position of editor to Webbe, Webbe apparently was dissatisfied with Franklin's proposition because he went to see Bradford. Bradford offered Webbe a more lucrative proposition, and Webbe accepted. Franklin inserted an advertisement about his magazine in the November 13, 1740, issue of the *Pennsylvania Gazette*:

> *In* January *next will be published,*
> (To be continued Monthly)
> The General Magazine,
> AND
> *Historical Chronicle,*
> For all the *British* Plantations in *America*:
> CONTAINING,

I. Extracts from the Votes, and Debates of the Parliament of *Great Britain.*

II. The Proclamations and Speeches of Governors; Addresses, Votes, Resolutions, &c. of Assemblies, in each Colony.

III. Accounts of, and Extracts from, all new Books, Pamphlets, &c. published in the Plantations.

IV. Essays, controversial, humorous, philosophical, religious, moral or political.

V. Select Pieces of Poetry.

VI. A concise CHRONICLE of the most remarkable Transactions, as well as in *Europe* as *America.*

VII. Births, Marriages, Deaths, and Promotions, of eminent Persons in the several Colonies.

VIII. Course of Exchange between the several Colonies, and *London*; Prices of Goods, &c.

This MAGAZINE, in Imitation of those in *England*, was long since projected; a Correspondence is settled with Intelligent Men in most of the Colonies, and small Types are procured, for carrying it on in the best Manner. It would not, indeed, have been published quite so soon, were it not that a Person, to whom the Scheme was communicated *in Confidence*, has thought fit to advertise it in the last *Mercury*, without our Participation; and, probably, with a View, by Starting before us, to discourage us from prosecuting our first Design, and reap the Advantage of it wholly to himself. We shall endeavour, however, by executing our Plan with Care, Diligence and Impartiality, and by Printing the Work neatly and correctly, to deserve a Share of the Publick Favour: But we desire no Subscriptions. We shall publish the Books at our own

Expence, and risque the Sale of them; which Method, we suppose, will be most agreeable to our Readers, as they will then be at Liberty to buy only what they like; and we shall be under a constant Necessity of endeavouring to make every particular Pamphlet worth their Money. Each Magazine shall contain four Sheets, of common sized Paper, in a small Character: Price *Six Pence* Sterling, or *Nine Pence Pennsylvania* Money; with considerable Allowance to Chapmen who take Quantities. To be printed and Sold by B. Franklin in *Philadelphia*.[43]

This advertisement apparently offended Webbe, because he wrote three articles that explained Franklin's proposition and his perspective toward it. The articles appeared in Bradford's newspaper, the *American Weekly Mercury*. Franklin ignored the first and second article, then responded to the third, which concerned Franklin's refusal, as postmaster, to have Bradford's newspaper delivered by the post office. Franklin, who had been instructed by the former postmaster general not to forward Bradford's newspaper because Bradford had been negligent in filing reports when he was postmaster, included the postmaster general's letter of instruction. Webbe responded to Franklin's rebuttal in a lengthy, two-page diatribe. The confrontation ended after Webbe's article, except for a humorous essay by Franklin that ridiculed Bradford's advertisement about his proposed magazine.[44]

Bradford's magazine lasted three issues. Franklin's magazine, which contained approximately 75 pages, lasted six issues. In the January 1741 issue, Franklin inserted the following advertisement:

Advertisement

THIS *Magazine* will be published Monthly, the Paper and Page will be continued of the same Size, that so the Twelve Months may be bound in one Volume at the Year's End, with a compleat Index or Table, which we shall add to the Month of *December*.

No Care shall be wanting, or Expence spared, to procure the best Materials for the Work, and make it as entertaining and useful as possible. The Character will generally be small, for the sake of comprising much in little Room, but it shall be good, and fairly printed.[45]

Franklin's magazine was the first of its kind to run an advertisement. Dated May 10, 1741, it appeared with the heading "ADVERTISEMENT," followed by:

Maryland, Charles County, May 10, 1741.

THere is a FERRY kept over Potomack, (by the Subscriber) being the Post Road, and much the nighest Way from Annapolis to Williamsburg, where all Gentlemen may depend upon a ready Passage in a good new Boat and able Hands. By Richard Brett, Deputy-Post-Master at Potomack.[46]

Franklin's magazine, like Bradford's, contained only one or two advertisements in any given issue, and these advertisements were usually announcements or notices of books or other magazines. Some advertisements informed readers in a simplistic manner about certain products such as inexpensive coffins, shoes, and cure-all compounds. The advertisements were brief and seldom contained ornaments or engravings. The purpose of Franklin's magazine was not to attract advertisers; James Playsted Wood stated that the purpose was "to present political information, knowledge of which he felt should be widespread among the thirteen colonies. To this end he devoted about a third of the space in his magazine to the reprinting of state papers."[47]

The American Magazine and Historical Chronicle, which was published in October 1743, was printed by Rogers and Fowle for Samuel Eliot and Joshua Blanchard in Boston. Containing 50 pages, the magazine imitated *The London Magazine* in its appearance. It contained a cut of Boston on the title page; *The London Magazine* contained a cut of London on its title page. The magazine contained advertisements, most notably about books "just published." The word "advertisement" was occasionally used. Beginning with the January 1746 issue, the word "advertisement" was printed in bold and preceded the advertisements, which, for the most part, concerned books.

In October 1757 in Philadelphia, William Bradford, Andrew Bradford's nephew, published *The American Magazine and Monthly Chronicle for the British Colonies*. The purpose of the magazine was to support England against France. The magazine's content reflected Philadelphia's culture.

The *Pennsylvania Magazine*, which began in January 1775, was published by Robert Aitkin and edited by Thomas Paine. The magazine contained a strong political bias. The magazine published the Declaration of Independence in its last issue, July 1776. Albert H. Smyth wrote that

Bradford's magazine had failed because of the imperfect communication between the colonies. Aitken's magazine, throughout its life of eighteen months, is overshadowed by the war, and the grave news successively reported from both sides of the ocean.[48]

The Columbian Magazine, or Monthly Miscellany was first published by Matthew Carey in October 1786. The magazine's contents included articles about politics, business, science, inventions, and agriculture—subjects that were popular among readers and therefore publishers of magazines. The magazine lasted until 1792. Carey also published *The American Magazine* from 1787 to 1792. Unlike *The Columbian*, which published original material, *The American Magazine* published writing that was worth preserving, including Thomas Paine's *Common Sense*. In addition to publishing writing about politics, the magazine carried articles on science, business, antislavery, education, and agriculture.

Isaiah Thomas, who published the *Massachusetts Spy*, founded the *Royal American Magazine* in 1774, the *Worcester Magazine* in 1786, and the *Massachusetts Magazine* in 1789. The first magazine ceased publication in 1775, while the second ceased publication in 1788. The latter, which carried articles about agriculture and business as well as fiction and poetry, ceased publication in 1796.

Although other magazines were founded, most lasted a few months. Advertisements were few and appeared on the last page or in supplements. Many issues of magazines carried no advertisements whatsoever. Therefore, publishers of magazines relied on subscribers to cover most, if not all, of their expenses. Unfortunately, some subscribers could not afford to pay; others paid periodically. As if this was not bad enough, certain publishers of magazines were handicapped by discriminating postal regulations. For instance, certain postmasters who published magazines refused to have other printers' publications delivered. This practice, which was common, applied to newspapers, too.

NOTES

1. *The Tatler*, No. 224, September 12–14, 1710.
2. Carl A. Bridenbaugh, *Cities in the Wilderness* (New York: Ronald Press Co., 1938), pp. 26–54.
3. E. R. Johnson et al., *History of Domestic and Foreign Commerce of the United States*, vol. 1 (Washington, D.C.: Carnegie Institution, 1915), pp. 162–174.
4. Bridenbaugh, *Cities in the Wilderness*, pp. 175–205.
5. Ibid., pp. 330–363.
6. Wilbur C. Plummer, "Consumer Credit in Colonial Philadelphia," *Pennsylvania Magazine of History and Biography*, Vol. 67 (October 1942), pp. 389–409.
7. John M. Blum et al., *The National Experience* (New York: Harcourt Brace Jovanovich, 1981), p. 64.
8. Ibid., p. 65.
9. J. A. Leo Lemay and P. M. Zall, eds., *The Autobiography of Benjamin Franklin: A Genetic Text* (Knoxville: University of Tennessee Press, 1981), p. 105.
10. Charles E. Clark, "The Newspapers of Provincial America," *Proceedings of the American Antiquarian Society*, vol. 100 (Worcester, Mass.: American Antiquarian Society, 1990), pp. 373–374.
11. *Boston News-Letter*, April 17–24, 1704.
12. *Boston News-Letter*, May 1–8, 1704.
13. Ibid.
14. *Boston News-Letter*, May 15–22, 1704.
15. *Boston News-Letter*, June 5–11, 1704.
16. *Boston News-Letter*, August 21, 1704.
17. Sidney Kobre, *The Development of the Colonial Newspaper* (Gloucester, Mass.: Peter Smith, 1960), p. 45.
18. Leonard W. Labaree et al., eds., *The Autobiography of Benjamin Franklin* by Benjamin Franklin (New Haven, Conn.: Yale University Press, 1964), p. 69.
19. *Pennsylvania Gazette*, September 25–October 2, 1729.
20. Ibid.
21. *Pennsylvania Gazette*, August 14–21, 1735.
22. *Pennsylvania Gazette*, June 23–30, 1737.
23. Ibid.
24. Ibid.

25. *Pennsylvania Gazette*, January 18–25, 1738, p. 9.

26. *Pennsylvania Gazette*, February 15–22, 1738, p. 9.

27. *Pennsylvania Gazette*, June 17, 1742.

28. In 1950 Benjamin Franklin was named a member of the Advertising Hall of Fame.

29. Benjamin Franklin, "Advice to a Young Tradesman, Written by an Old One. To My Friend A. B.," *The Instructor: Or Young Man's Best Companion*, 9th ed. revised and corrected, ed. George Fisher (Philadelphia: B. Franklin and D. Hall, 1748), p. 375. Also cited in Leonard W. Labaree, ed., and Whitfield J. Bell, Jr., associate ed., *The Papers of Benjamin Franklin, Vol. 3: January 1, 1745, through June 30, 1750* (New Haven, Conn.: Yale University Press, 1961), p. 306.

30. *New York Gazette*, October 3–10, 1737.

31. *New York Gazette*, September 26–October 3, 1737.

32. *New York Gazette*, November 14–21, 1737.

33. Quoted in Frank Presbrey, *The History and Development of Advertising* (Garden City, N.Y.: Doubleday, 1929), p. 142.

34. *New-York Weekly Journal*, March 29, 1736.

35. Isaiah Thomas, *The History of Printing in America, with a Biography of Printers in Two Volumes* (New York: Burt Franklin, n.d.; originally published in 1874), pp. 8–9.

36. William A. Dill, *Growth of Newspapers in the United States* (Lawrence: Department of Journalism, University of Kansas, 1928), p. 11.

37. Sidney Kobre, "The Revolutionary Colonial Press—A Social Interpretation," *Journalism Quarterly*, Vol. 20, No. 3 (September 1943), pp. 198–199.

38. Ibid., p. 196.

39. Ronald Hoffman, "The Press in Mercantile Maryland: A Question of Utility," *Journalism Quarterly*, Vol. 46, No. 3 (Autumn 1969), pp. 536–537.

40. James M. Lee, *History of American Journalism* (Garden City, N.Y.: Garden City Publishing Co., 1917), p. 94.

41. Louis B. Wright, *The Cultural Life of the American Colonies 1607–1763* (New York: Harper and Brothers, 1957).

42. James Playsted Wood, *The Story of Advertising* (New York: Ronald Press Co., 1958), p. 65.

43. *Pennsylvania Gazette*, November 13, 1740.

44. Lyon N. Richardson, *A History of Early American Magazines 1741–1789* (New York: Octagon Books, 1966; originally published by Thomas Nelson and Sons, 1931), pp. 17–25.

45. *The General Magazine and Historical Chronicle, for All the British Plantations in America* (January 1741).

46. *The General Magazine and Historical Chronicle, for All the British Plantations in America* (May 1741).

47. James Playsted Wood, *Magazines in the United States*, 3d ed. (New York: Ronald Press Co., 1971), p. 13.

48. Albert H. Smyth, *The Philadelphia Magazines and Their Contributors 1741–1850* (Freeport, N.Y.: Books for Libraries Press, 1970; originally published in 1892), pp. 52–53.

2

The First Advertising Agents

INTRODUCTION

America became 13 states, with each state having a written constitution. The Articles of Confederation, which went into effect in 1781, represented the nation; reforms were made by the states. The Constitution reflected capitalism, and the framers of the document were certainly familiar with Adam Smith's book, *The Wealth of Nations*, which was published in 1776 and which emphasized a "society of perfect liberty." Smith realized that economic growth occurred in free and open societies.[1]

The nation struggled to form a democracy, but lives had been lost, and the country's economy was plagued by inflation and debt. When taxes were implemented, certain citizens rebelled. Since the nation's central government was practically powerless—the Articles of Confederation failed to give Congress the power to enforce or enact certain laws, particularly taxation—the country suffered for several years.

By 1790, however, the economic picture of America had improved. Congress had passed the Northwest Ordinance in 1787, an act that encouraged Americans to purchase acreage inland and, as a result, brought the nation thousands of dollars from sales. A Constitution that gave Congress the power it desperately needed was endorsed by representatives of the states a year later, and a new Congress was elected. The Bill of Rights, which contained 10 amendments, was added to the Constitution in 1791. During the French Revolution, France claimed that America was bound by the Franco-American Alliance of 1778 to support it in its war against England and other European nations. George Washington, who had become the nation's first president, declared neutrality, basically for monetary reasons, since England purchased most of America's exports. Of course, France grew furious when a treaty between the United States and England was signed and ratified. Though Washington's efforts were for the welfare of the nation, his action did not go unopposed. For instance, Thomas Jefferson and other Republicans disliked the treaty for its favoritism. The press was divided over the issue. Political upheaval lasted 30 years.

In 1798, when John Adams was president, France declared war against the United States. Fortunately, France was too involved in Europe to do any harm. After a few battles at sea, France agreed to negotiate peace. Though Adams had tasted victory and had increased his popularity with the voters, his break with Hamilton split the party, and Jefferson was elected president.

Jefferson saw the need to acquire land; in 1803 he purchased the Louisiana territory. He tried to obtain Florida but failed. Because of his and perhaps his cabinet's hands-off attitude toward England and France, America's relations with both degenerated. Madison attempted to gain respect from both countries, but relations grew exceedingly worse. In 1812 Madison and Congress declared war against England. The war lasted two years. What happened abroad affected the United States. Since France had owned parts of America, and since England had at one time ruled the colonies, each country deemed it necessary to keep or recover what each had. Perhaps England, since it had crushed France's military forces, was convinced that it could pressure the United States—it had fired upon several ships that belonged to the U.S. Navy—into paying tariffs on overseas shipping. England lost the war, however.

The United States continued to grow. By 1821 six states had been added to the Union. During the 1820s and 1830s, public offices that had been appointive became elective. Voting increased as a result of fewer restrictions. An ideal democracy like none that man had witnessed materialized when Andrew Jackson's Democratic Party rivaled the revered Republican and, later, Whig parties. Jackson's leadership, which had been displayed at the Battle of New Orleans, captured the nation's attention. He opposed a high tariff, a new Bank of the United States, federal reapportionment of House seats, and distribution of land revenues to the states; he approved of westward and southward expansion, a strong foreign policy, and an independent treasury.

When John Tyler, a Whig, was elected in 1840, the expansion movement continued, and when James K. Polk was elected four years later, he secured the northwest territory, particularly Oregon, and the southwest territory, which had been part of Mexico.

The Americans who inhabited the Republic of Texas had slaves. Since Texas was then under the Mexican government, and since that government prohibited slavery, the clash led to revolution. When the United States attempted to annex Texas in 1845, Mexico declared war. Within three years Mexico had not only lost the war but sold Texas, Northern California, and New Mexico to the United States.

Slavery was becoming an issue in the United States, especially in the North, where the practice was frowned upon by politicians, professional people, and newspaper publishers and editors. Other problems, such as the various movements that shaped public opinion, and sectional loyalty, which prejudiced members of certain groups or areas of the country, did not help the situation. When Stephen A. Douglas' Kansas-Nebraska bill, which allowed slavery in territory that had been reserved for free states, appeared in 1854, northerners against slavery created the new Republican Party. Although the party's candidate for president, John C. Fremont, lost the election in 1856, he received most of the votes cast in the free states.

In 1860, after Abraham Lincoln won the presidential election, the South seceded from the Union and in 1861 founded its own government, headed by Jefferson Davis. The same year the Confederates fired on supply ships enroute to Fort Sumter, which started the Civil War. The Union, made up of 23 states, had advantages over the 11 Confederate states. The Union had twice as many inhabitants, more manufacturing firms, and more railroads. Emancipation of the slaves did not become an official federal issue until 1862, when President Lincoln issued his proclamation, which Congress failed to enact until after the war. Although Lincoln's popularity increased after the taking of Atlanta, his administration suffered severe criticism. This was also true of Davis and his administration. The leaders in the southern states realized that slavery had to be abolished to survive. Southerners living in the North, on the other hand, cared little for emancipation of the slaves. By the time the war ended, both sides had suffered. Reconstruction, which was approached differently by President Lincoln and the Congress, created as many problems as the war, politically speaking. When Lincoln was assassinated, Andrew Johnson, a southerner, became president. His plans for Reconstruction, which pardoned Confederates and belittled African Americans, allowed the southern states to govern themselves as long as their allegiance was to the Union. Black Codes were enacted in these states to regulate the freedom of former slaves. Such legislation caused political opposition in Washington between the Republicans in Congress and the president. Eventually, differences and actions caused the Congress to impeach the president; he was acquitted by the Senate by a margin of one vote.

In 1868 Ulysses Grant was elected president. Although he served two terms, scandal marred his presidency. Rutherford B. Hayes, a moderate Republican who tried to help restore the South's economic climate by providing federal subsidies, was elected president. Hayes, who tried to implement federal measures that would make southern elections open to African Americans as well as whites, was pressured into withdrawing the measures. Subsequently, African Americans were eliminated from voter registrations. State after state enacted laws that required African Americans to be literate to vote. Consequently, African Americans became segregated.

Throughout the latter 1800s the South suffered. Whites were as poor as African Americans. In fact, the southern states ranked the lowest in every statistical index.

In 1880 James A. Garfield, another Republican, became president, but he was murdered a year later. His successor, Chester A. Arthur, endorsed the Pendleton Civil Service Act in 1883. This act established a Civil Service Commission, which administered examinations to both prospective employees and employees of the government. Grover Cleveland, the first Democrat to be elected president in 25 years, was elected in 1884. Cleveland faced a divided Congress; however, he used the president's power of veto on any bill he deemed wasteful. In addition, western land that had been fraudulently obtained was restored to the public domain. The Interstate Commerce Act, which was enacted to legislate corrupt practices made by railroads, was enacted in 1887.

The Republicans returned to power in 1888, when Benjamin Harrison became president. Congress, too, was controlled by the Republicans. Thus, it was rather easy for the Sherman Anti-Trust Act, which stipulated that monopolies restraining trade between states or foreign countries were illegal, to be enacted in 1890. However, it was not used to break up an industrial monopoly until 10 years later. The McKinley Tariff, which was designed to attract farmers by protecting certain agricultural products, actually increased tariff schedules, which subsequently raised prices on goods purchased by farmers. Instead of helping farmers the measures only ignited Farmers' Alliances, which engaged in politics.

Grover Cleveland, as a result of indifferences between political parties principally caused by the McKinley Tariff, won the presidential election in 1892. The country faced an economic depression. The cattle industry had been severely curtailed in 1887 by a blizzard; farming was paralyzed; industrialists suffered; and the Sherman Silver Purchasing Act of 1890 was draining the nation's gold supply. Cleveland forced Congress to repeal the act in 1893.

William McKinley, a Republican who was elected over William Jennings Bryan in 1896, signed the Dingley Tariff Act, which increased duties on imports in 1897. The production of gold increased, and the Gold Standard Act, which was enacted in 1900, required the Treasury to maintain a minimum gold reserve. Before 1900 prosperity returned to the farmer and the industrialist. Financial support for industrial expansion was available from such financiers as J. P. Morgan.

In 1898 the Spanish-American War occurred after the *Maine*

was sunk in Havana Harbor. Promoted by William Randolph Hearst's *New York American* and Joseph Pulitzer's *New York World*, the war was over within weeks.

During the 1800s, the United States progressed at a remarkable rate. In 1800 the principal forms of retailing included general stores, markets, and peddlers. General stores were prevalent, and the majority of merchants sold at wholesale and retail. Eventually, retailing leaned toward specialization by merchandise lines or by function. Advertising by merchants stressed the availability of products rather than products' attributes. The source of the merchandise was given, as was the amount on hand. However, retail advertising, at least in its early days, rarely contained prices.[2]

The selling agent came into his own before 1860, providing a broad range of services to manufacturers, including sales assistance, market information, and advice regarding which means of transportation should be employed. Many selling agents owned stock in manufacturing firms and consequently had considerable influence on managerial decisions.[3]

Commerce gave rise to regional specialization and contributed to the growth of cities. By 1860 the nation had prospered to the extent that it no longer depended on Europe to purchase its goods. Innovations in technology helped increase production, especially in textiles. Industrial workers formed unions because of exploitation. Banks increased in number. Transportation projects such as canals, steamboats, and turnpikes advanced and helped reduce costs of certain products. According to George Rogers Taylor, the rapid development of a national transportation system made interregional trade economically feasible.[4] In the South cotton became the chief asset. In the North factories supported employees who lived in cities. For most of the nation's citizenry agriculture was the primary means of livelihood.

Immigrants from the Old World, including England, Ireland, and Germany, arrived daily. Immigrants from Germany fared well, while those from Ireland fared poorly. Germans, who had money or access to financial aid, purchased farms. The Irish, for the most part, congregated in cities, where they worked at low-paying jobs. Usually, because of their low wages, they had to live in slums filled with pestilence and disease. African Americans, even those who lived in the North, were worse off, for they had to take jobs that whites refused. In addition, most faced hostility from whites almost every day. Freedom for many of them was merely a word.

City government, in order to survive and expand its obligations to the citizenry, was forced to tax. Police forces came into existence, garbage was removed, streets were undeniably improved, and education progressed.

Religion, similar to what was happening in Europe, witnessed a rise in interdenominational revivalism before 1840. City after city received scores of ministers who believed that cities were the dens where Satan dwelled.

As the country progressed, so did its citizenry. Wealth was obtained by a select few, however. Various movements, on the other hand, affected more people. These movements, which swept across the country, were created by certain groups for certain issues, such as women's rights, capital punishment, workers' rights, education, mental health, temperance, and pacifism. Abolitionism was the most controversial. Other movements, which included communistic communities such as Brook Farm, were not as popular as their promoters hoped.

The nation's population increased, and when 9 million immigrants entered the nation in the late 1800s, citizens of America grew concerned. The western territory was settled and eventually gained statehood. Silver as well as gold was discovered. Cattle became an industry not only in Texas but in the Dakotas. Railroads branched from the East and the West, and in 1869 one complete line crossed the American landscape. Unfortunately, owners of railroads realized their power; consequently, they fixed prices, they monopolized transportation, they discriminated against certain customers, and they used their power to influence local and state legislators and subsequent legislation.

The Native American was pushed aside until federal legislation intervened.

Industry, which had grown from the beginning of the century, more than doubled in production between the late 1870s and the 1890s. Production of iron and steel in the United States, unlike the rest of the world, increased. The telephone, phonograph, electric light bulb, and typewriter, among other inventions, spawned new industries. Petroleum used for engines as well as heating and lighting created another major industry.

Industries led to the creation of trusts, which were monopolies, by John D. Rockefeller and others. Company mergers also appeared. Tensions between management and employees ensued; subsequently, laborers formed more unions, a few of which became national in size. Through strikes and boycotts labor tried to obtain higher wages, better working conditions, and fewer hours. Before the turn of the century, because of several incidents in which people were either injured or killed, labor unions received severe criticism from the press and the public.

The advocacy and muckraking journalists reported vividly the opening of the West, the wars between the United States and its adversaries, and the unscrupulous practices by managers and owners of large companies, especially monopolies.

In this climate of change the first advertising agents appeared. Ralph M. Hower reported that advertising agencies passed through four stages before N. W. Ayer and Son was founded. The first stage was the newspaper agency, which was inaugurated by Volney B. Palmer, who represented newspaper publishers. The second stage occurred in the 1850s, when agents became independent. Space-jobbing, as this stage was called, became popular as agents realized they could earn more by selling space to advertisers. This stage caused many agents to question their role. After all, they did not work for publishers, and they did not work for advertisers. Yet, they referred to themselves as agents. The third stage developed out of the second when George P. Rowell purchased large amounts of space in newspapers, then resold it in small amounts to advertisers. This stage, which has been called space-wholesaling, began in 1865. The fourth stage was based on Rowell's idea and appeared in the late 1860s. Called the advertising concession agency, this stage occurred when Carlton and Smith (later, the J. Walter Thompson Company) purchased most—if not all—of the advertising space in certain publications for a specified period of time. Consequently, the agency, not the publisher, was responsible for securing advertisers for the entire publication. This practice actually closed the gap between agent and publisher, but the agent worked as an independent middleman nonetheless.[5]

VOLNEY B. PALMER

Volney B. Palmer, who had offices in Boston, New York, Baltimore, and Philadelphia, was a pioneer. He was the first advertising agent, and he represented more newspapers than did other agents of his day. In addition, he promoted advertising as an integral part of marketing and produced as well as delivered advertisements to publishers.

Palmer was born to Nathan and Jerusha Palmer in Wilkes-Barre, Pennsylvania, in 1799. His father, a lawyer who held several political positions in Wilkes-Barre, moved his wife and six children to Mount Holly, New Jersey, in 1818, where he published the *Burlington Mirror*, a newspaper on which every member of the family worked. He changed the name of the newspaper to the *New Jersey Mirror and Burlington County Advertiser* about a year later. The newspaper continued to be popular among readers and advertisers, even after Nathan's death in 1842, when it was published by his widow, then his daughter, Eliza.

Palmer and one of his four brothers moved to Pottsville, Pennsylvania, in 1830, where he invested and worked in real estate. In 1841, after he married, Palmer moved his family to Philadelphia, where he attempted to sell real estate in an economically depressed city. By 1842 he had added a coal office as well as an advertising business to his real estate venture, as the following advertisement illustrates:

V. B. Palmer's
REAL ESTATE AND COAL OFFICE
No. 104 South Third Street
(a few doors below the Exchange)
Philadelphia

Agency for the Purchase and Sale of Houses and Lots, Farms, Farming, Timber and Coal Lands, Bonds and Mortgages, Ground Rents, Anthracite Coal, &c.

ADVERTISEMENTS and Subscriptions received from some of the best and most widely circulated newspapers in Pennsylvania and New Jersey, and in many of the principal cities and towns throughout the United States, for which he has the agency, affording an excellent op-

portunity for Merchants, Mechanics, Professional Men, Hotel and
Boarding House Keepers, Railroad, Insurance and Transportation Companies, and the enterprising portion of the community generally, to publish extensively abroad their respective pursuits—to learn the terms of
subscription and advertising, and accomplish their object here without
the trouble of perplexing and fruitless inquiries, the expense and labor
of letter writing; the risk of making enclosures of money &c, &c.[6]

Palmer remained in real estate for the next several years, even
though his advertising interests were fruitful. In 1849 he used
"Advertising Agency" in an advertisement for the first time. He
claimed to be the sole representative of 1,300 newspapers. This,
Palmer realized, allowed advertisers to be selective. In addition,
Palmer created speculative presentations for these prospective
advertisers. The advertiser was informed of the total cost, not
just the space rates for each newspaper selected. Palmer received
a 25 percent commission from the publisher upon payment. The
commission system is used today, except that agencies usually
receive 15 percent, not 25.

Palmer provided a number of services besides those mentioned. According to his *Almanac* of 1850:

- he is Agent for the best papers of every section of the whole country.
- he is empowered by the proprietors to make contracts and give receipts.
- his long experience and practical knowledge qualify him to give valuable information.
- the same prices only are charged to advertisers as are exacted by his
  principals, the publishers.
- a selection can be made suitably adapted to the various pursuits of
  advertisers.
- a complete system of advertising can be adapted upon either a large
  or small scale.
- the papers are on file at the Agency, where advertisers can examine
  them, see the terms, and obtain all requisite information to enable
  them to advertise judiciously, effectively and safely.[7]

From the preceding it is easy to ascertain that Palmer's agency
did more for advertisers than most agencies at the time. Palmer

promoted his services by using endorsements from publishers. According to Donald R. Holland, Palmer "urged business men to use advertising on a regular basis, to use it to develop new markets, to take advantage of the flexibility of advertising to specific regions or in specific seasons."[8]

By the mid-1850s, Palmer was considered by numerous clients as a godsend, and his agency grew. He opened four offices in four major cities. He maintained the office in Philadelphia and hired others to manage the other three. He visited the other offices at various times throughout each year.

In the late 1850s, John E. Joy, W. W. Sharpe, and J. E. Coe became partners. When Palmer retired in either 1862 or 1863, Joy and Coe operated the Philadelphia and the New York offices, respectively. The latter office was eventually purchased by W. W. Sharpe. The office in Boston was controlled by S. R. Niles.

Palmer died in 1864; he was 65. Palmer helped advertisers and newspaper publishers. He sold the idea of advertising to advertisers and consequently made hundreds of proprietors realize how important a role advertising played in a capitalistic society.

S. M. Pettengill, who had worked for Palmer, described him as

a short, thick-set gentleman of good address, genial and pleasant in manner, and had a good command of language, full of wise saws and modern instances. He was a capital story-teller, wore gold spectacles and carried a gold-headed cane, and was a first-rate canvasser. He had more self-possession and assurance than any man I ever knew.[9]

GEORGE P. ROWELL

George P. Rowell was born in 1838 in Concord, Vermont, to Samuel and Caroline Rowell. When he was a teenager, he moved with his parents to a farm outside Lancaster, New Hampshire. Rowell, who was studious, attended Lancaster Academy. At 17 he left home to pursue employment in Boston. He taught school for several years, then worked in a store until the recession of 1857.

Rowell found employment with the *Boston Post*, for which he eventually sold space to advertisers. Rowell was working at the paper when he married Sarah Eastman in 1862. Although Rowell earned enough to support his family, in 1864 he created a theatrical playbill for which he sold space to advertisers. He continued the playbill for several weeks and as a result of the advertising netted a comfortable profit.

In 1865 he left the *Post* and opened an advertising agency with his friend Horace Dodd. They devised a "list system" of newspapers for advertisers to consider. Unlike Palmer, they purchased large quantities of column space from these newspapers, then sold the space in small quantities to advertisers. In short, they purchased space at wholesale, then sold it at retail. They persuaded certain publishers to give them a discount based on continued patronage. The agents received an additional 3 percent off the card rate if they paid in cash within a 30-day period. The agents did not have to pay more than 25 percent of the card rate for most of the newspapers they handled. Rowell was responsible for the cash discount in addition to the commission.

Rowell's "list system" became instantly popular and was adopted by other agencies. Rowell and Dodd started the *Advertisers' Gazette*, a house organ that promoted advertising and the agency.

Rowell sold the agency to Dodd in 1867 and moved his family to New York, which had become the most important commercial city in the nation because of its location. By 1860 New York handled more than 65 percent of the country's imports and more than 30 percent of its exports, and because of its easy access the city appealed to western markets.[10]

Rowell established the agency George P. Rowell and Company and continued using the "list system," which was criticized by S. M. Pettengill, a competitor, at a New York State Editorial Association meeting:

Mr. Pettengill . . . berated the publishers for their lack of business methods, and took special exception to the practice, of which many of them were guilty, of selling to Mr. Rowell . . . a column of space at a yearly rate, and allowing him to peddle it out to monthly users of an inch, more or less, at less than half the price the publisher would demand of the advertiser, . . . and much worse than that, at less than half the price the same publisher would demand from him, Pettengill, if he, instead of Rowell, should happen to send the same care of an inch or thereabouts to appear for a single month.[11]

Rowell happened to be in the audience and realized that Pettengill considered him a competitor, even though Pettengill had been in business longer. Rowell and Pettengill became friends primarily as a result of their professional interests. Rowell made an effort to make sure that circulation figures claimed by publishers were accurate. As he candidly pointed out in an agency flyer:

In fixing the value of advertising space in any particular journal, the first question to be considered is the number of copies issued; next the character or quality of the circulation.

A well-printed paper is worth more than one badly printed; an influential journal carries more weight than one without reputation.

So also a paper which habitually charges high prices for its advertising thereby makes its columns exclusive, and will have fewer, and as a rule, a better class of advertisements, and is worth something more on that account.

The value of all these considerations is recognized, but exactly *how* much each one is to be considered becomes a question of judgment.[12]

Rowell realized that if his agency could supply the preceding to advertisers, then advertisers would know how much to pay for the space they purchased. As Rowell pointed out, that was one purpose of his agency.

Rowell continued to publish the house organ, *Advertisers' Gazette*, which was mentioned earlier, and in 1869, as a service to prospective advertisers, he published the first volume of *Rowell's American Newspaper Directory*, which listed more than 5,000 newspapers in the United States and more than 300 in Canada that the agency handled and, of course, various advertisements, which defrayed part of the publication cost. Although Rowell had tried to eliminate so-called private lists, he was criticized by other agents for making available at a nominal cost more information than they offered. Rowell had misgivings about the directory because it disclosed information about newspapers that other agencies did not have. Rowell was also criticized by publishers for printing conservative circulation figures of their respective newspapers. Yet, these publishers accepted advertising from his agency. The publication was updated and issued annually. As a result of this publication, publishers of newspapers eventually changed their circulation figures.

Rowell also published the *American Newspaper Reporter*, which was a house organ that preceded *Printers' Ink*. The organ contained insightful features about individuals who worked in the advertising and newspaper businesses, as well as other informative articles. In the November 20, 1871, issue, he wrote about "The Principles of Advertising":

Honesty is by all odds the very strongest point which can be crowded into an advertisement. Come right down with the facts, boldly, firmly, unflinchingly. Say directly what it is, what it has done, what it will do. Leave out all ifs. Do not claim too much, but what you do claim must be claimed without the smallest shadow of weakness. Do not say "we are convinced that," "we believe that" or "ours is among the best" or "equal to any" or "surpassed by none." Say flatly "the best," or say nothing. Do not refer to rivals. Ignore every person, place or thing except yourself, your address and your article. . . . Be serious and dignified, but active and lively. Leave wit, however good it may be, entirely aside.[13]

Rowell realized that advertising copy, which suffered from too many words—that is, overstatement—needed improving. He also realized that every advertisement—even small ones—had to attract attention.

By 1871 Rowell's "list system" had been employed six years and had proved profitable. Rowell himself had accumulated more than $100,000. Yet, the firm continued to add to its various lists of newspapers and clients. Rowell's firm placed numerous advertisements for various questionable remedies, for instance, even though Rowell's opinion toward advertising patent medicine changed dramatically years later.

Rowell's success, which had come at an early age, allowed him to take four months of vacation, which he did almost every year beginning in 1871. The same year he decided to share the agency's profits with his employees, a practice that Rowell continued, but with some regret.

In 1878 Rowell issued a small pamphlet that expressed the principles and conditions that guided the agency. The following paragraph from the booklet summarized the purpose for the George P. Rowell and Company's existence:

Our Newspaper Advertising Bureau . . . is an establishment intended to facilitate the convenient and systematic placing of advertisements in newspapers. It is conducted upon the principles which we conceive to be the right ones for securing the best results to the advertiser, the publisher, and ourselves.[14]

The same year Rowell sold the firm's house organ, the *American Newspaper Reporter and Advertisers' Gazette*, to R. H. C. Valentine, who changed the subhead and design. The publication ceased after several issues, however.

In 1880 Rowell purchased "Prospect Farm" in New Hampshire and seldom worked in advertising. The farm did not occupy all of his time, however. In addition to traveling abroad, he fished, unsuccessfully sought public office, and published a small and unprofitable newspaper.

Rowell returned to his office in New York in 1888 and published *Printers' Ink*. Rowell wrote, "I had always an itching to have a mouth-piece through which I could speak to those whose interests were in lines parallel to mine."[15] The purpose of *Printers' Ink*, then, was to discuss the business of advertising. The publication became a journal for advertisers and was so successful commercially that eventually it had at least 200 imitations.

In 1890 Rowell's marriage ended in divorce; he married Jeannette Hallock several months later in 1891.

In 1892 he sold the firm to several employees. Unfortunately, within several years the investors owed newspaper publishers more than they had received from advertisers, and Rowell purchased the company for one dollar and assumed all debts.

In 1905 Rowell retired from advertising and wrote 52 papers about his life and experiences in advertising. These papers appeared in *Printers' Ink*, then in the book *Forty Years an Advertising Agent: 1865–1905*, which was published in 1906.

Rowell died at Poland Springs, Maine, in 1908. His annual newspaper directory was purchased the same year by the N. W.

Ayer and Son advertising agency, which published the *N. W. Ayer and Son's American Newspaper Annual.*

Regarding the operation of an advertising agency, Rowell wrote that

it is one of the easiest sorts of business in which a man may cheat and defraud a client without danger of discovery; and also note that no agent who was not superior to this temptation has ever been permanently successful. The high reputation for honor and probity uniformly enjoyed by those who have been most conspicuous in the business has been gained by strict integrity—a determination to secure a fair deal for every patron.[16]

N. W. AYER AND SON

Francis Wayland Ayer was influenced by the four stages discussed earlier when he opened his advertising agency in Philadelphia in 1868.

Ayer, who was born in 1848 in Lee, Massachusetts, was influenced, too, by his father, Nathan Wheeler Ayer. N. W. Ayer, a graduate of Brown University, named his son after Dr. Francis Wayland, one of Brown's presidents. Joanna B. Ayer, his mother, died when Ayer was three. N. W. Ayer, a devout Baptist, married Harriet Post when his son was six. N. W. Ayer practiced law for several years in Massachusetts, taught in Massachusetts and New York, then purchased a seminary in Philadelphia in 1867. He was not successful financially. He earned a modest living until he suffered from ill health.

Francis Wayland Ayer learned from his father the basic principles that helped him throughout his life. He knew what responsibility, integrity, and honesty meant. His value system was never questioned. When he was 14, he taught in a country school in New York. A year later he was offered a position in a village school. For the next several years one promotion followed another. He desired to go to college, however, and in 1867 he attended the University of Rochester. Within a year he had spent his savings. Although he asked his father for help, his father was barely earning an income. F. W. Ayer left the university in search of a job. The publisher of the *National Baptist*, a weekly religious newspaper, hired him to solicit advertisements. Ayer earned $1,200 in commissions in less than a year. His employer offered him $2,000 a year to stay with the firm. Ayer refused the opportunity. He was certain he could earn more on his own. He persuaded his father to work with him, and on April 1, 1869, he opened the agency N. W. Ayer and Son. He named the agency after his father for several reasons: he admired his father; his father agreed to work with him; and the name sounded more impressive than just F. W. Ayer.

The Ayer agency began with 11 religious newspapers. Like other agents of his day, Ayer solicited advertisements from advertisers, then placed them in the publications listed with his agency. In addition, he purchased the total advertising space in certain publications, then resold it in partials to advertisers. Thus, he acted as manager of advertising departments of some publications. Ayer also placed advertisements in publications that were not on his list. In such instances, he estimated how much the space would cost, then quoted a price that was slightly higher than his estimated cost to advertisers. Ayer earned income the best way he knew how: by selling and bargaining. There was little time for experimenting, especially during the agency's formative years. By the end of its first year, the agency represented more than 11 newspapers. Growth continued, and in 1870 Ayer had to move to a larger office and hire his first employee, George O. Wallace, a bookkeeper.

Within two years, the agency had to move again. It was handling more than 300 publications located in 27 of the 37 states that made up the nation. In addition, advertisements for clients were placed in other publications through other agents.

In 1873 N. W. Ayer died. Francis purchased his father's interest in the business. His stepmother, Harriet Post, did not have the experience or the inclination to be a partner. Ayer reasoned that absentee ownership would not be beneficial to current and prospective clients. The same year, as a result of growth, Ayer asked Wallace to become a partner; Wallace accepted a one-fourth interest in the firm.

Throughout the 1870s the Ayer agency grew. By 1876 it could place advertisements in any newspaper published in the United States or Canada, because Ayer had created a printing department a year earlier so the agency could print most of the advertisements in-house. This gave the agency an advantage over other agencies; most agencies hired independent printers to print their clients' advertisements.

In 1877 the firm purchased Coe, Wetherill and Company, another agency in Philadelphia. Coe, Wetherill and Company had succeeded Joy, Coe and Company, which had acquired Palmer's agency. In addition, the agency, like Rowell's, published *Ayer and Son's Manual for Advertisers*, primarily to promote its list of publications, and, later, *The Advertiser's Guide*, a quarterly magazine filled with informative features and promotional pieces about advertising.

In the mid-1870s, Ayer, like other agencies, placed advertisements for makers of patent medicine. Some of these included Compound Oxygen, Kennedy's Ivory Tooth Cement, Rock and Rye, and Dr. Case's Liver Remedy and Blood Purifier. Other firms were represented, too, including John Wanamaker, Montgomery Ward and Company, Whitman's Chocolates, Blackwell's Durham smoking tobacco, and Singer sewing machines. Ayer also represented manufacturers of farm machinery as well as educational institutions such as Harvard College.

During this time Ayer analyzed Rowell's methods of handling publishers and clients and realized that Rowell had put himself in the middle—that is, he was being paid by the publisher, yet he was representing the advertiser. How could Rowell serve both?, Ayer wondered. Ayer decided to represent the advertiser. Unlike Rowell, he would inform an advertiser as to how much space cost. Furthermore, he would inform an advertiser as to what the agency received for its services. Instead of being merely a space-seller like other agencies, Ayer's agency would become a space-buyer and therefore be paid by the client. Ayer believed this plan was fair to the client and actually superior to Rowell's plan.

The Ayer open-contract-plus-commission plan was initiated in late 1875, the year he married Rhandeena Gilman. Through trial and error, Ayer learned how to earn a profit from his commission system. This was not as difficult as persuading advertisers to look at advertising from a different perspective. The advertiser had to trust Ayer, and vice versa. Ayer would buy space at the lowest possible cost for the advertiser. The advertiser would have access to Ayer's lists of rates. Thus, the advertiser could determine the cost of advertising space in a specific publication and, consequently, the commission to the agency. This system allowed Ayer to buy advertising space wisely as well as consider the advertiser's needs, which are hallmarks of modern agencies. The system, although sound, was not adopted by every agency that learned about it, but it forced every agency to recognize that advertisers had interests that needed servicing and, to a certain extent, protecting.

In 1878 Ayer allowed Henry Nelson McKinney to become a partner. McKinney, an expert in sales, believed in the power of advertising and in the open-contract system. He was extremely important to the growth of the agency.

In 1879 Ayer started another service when it conducted a market survey of the nation to entice the Nichols-Shepard Company, which manufactured threshing machines. The survey presented the production of grains by counties and states. In addition, the agency included an in-depth advertising plan. This is the first advertising campaign based on a market survey. The company hired Ayer as a result of the survey, and Ayer realized that this particular service could be performed for other advertisers. By 1900 the agency was preparing advertising plans for every client.

In 1880 the agency focused on writing advertising copy in addition to printing advertisements:

The Composition, Illustration and Display of Newspaper Advertisements has so long been a study with us that we have become admittedly expert in preparing the best possible effects.

Having at command the services of an Artist, a Wood Engraver, and a number of Printers who have been for years engaged almost exclusively in this work under our direction, we possess entirely unequaled facilities for serving those who desire to entrust their business to our care.[17]

During the same year the agency published the *American Newspaper Annual*, which listed every newspaper and magazine published in the United States and Canada. This annual later became the *N. W. Ayer and Son's Directory of Newspapers and Pe-*

riodicals, which is still published but under a different title. Revenue from the annual was from advertising placed by newspaper publishers.

Ayer's business policy changed in the 1880s. For instance, the agency refused advertising that would discredit the agency or would disappoint the advertiser. In 1887 Ayer presented his agency's philosophy in a circular:

We do not wish any advertising which cannot reasonably be expected to *pay the advertiser.*

We do not wish any advertiser to deal with us unless it is to *his interest to do so.*

We always say just what we believe, even though we have to advise a man not to spend any money in newspaper advertising.

We aim to give as conscientious consideration to little as to larger matters. Small orders entrusted to us receive just as careful attention as the largest ones get.

We thoroughly believe in newspaper advertising, and that there is more value in it than most people think. We therefore contend that the subject deserves an intelligent and unprejudiced consideration, to which should be applied as good business sense as any other matter of business commands.

We are not anxious for any order with which there does not come the reasonable expectation, *first*, that the advertising will pay our customer; and *again*, that we can so handle the business as to convince him that his interests will be best served by entrusting to us all his future advertising orders.[18]

Most of the advertising handled by the agency in the 1880s came from small businesses, such as retail stores, and from schools and colleges. The agency handled large accounts, too, such as Hires' root beer, J. I. Case threshing machines, and Procter & Gamble soaps. As early as 1891, the agency added the N. K. Fairbanks Company, which produced soaps, and Mellin's Baby Food. From 1894 to 1898, the agency's clients were affected by the recession. When businesses expanded in the late 1890s, so did Ayer. For instance, it handled advertising for Standard Oil and several of its subsidiaries. In 1899 it handled the major campaign that introduced the Uneeda Biscuit, which was sold in individual, airtight packages. The campaign, which was for the

National Biscuit Company and was the largest up to that time, included newspaper, magazine, and outdoor advertisements. The campaign was an overwhelming success. With the clients that have been mentioned, Ayer could stop handling beer and whiskey accounts altogether as well as curtail patent medicine accounts. In 1896 beer advertising was dropped. Three years later whiskey advertising was halted. Patent medicine advertising was stopped in the early 1900s.

In 1898 Ayer promoted Jarvis A. Wood, who had supervised the copy department and had managed numerous employees in the agency, and Albert G. Bradford, who had supervised the space-buying department, to partners. Ayer realized that he and McKinney could not manage the growth of the agency by themselves.

Ayer realized before 1900 that advertising specific brands was just as important as advertising new products. He made certain that businesses were aware of this as well in 1900, when he conducted a massive campaign for the agency.

By 1900 Ayer saw his agency grow into the largest in the nation, with more than 160 employees and profits exceeding $58,000. In 1902 the agency moved because of needed space. Ayer opened branch offices in New York in 1903, Boston in 1905, Chicago in 1910, and Cleveland in 1911.[19]

Ayer realized that the agency had become too large to manage, even for himself and the partners. None of the partners knew enough about every aspect of the agency to manage it properly, and he was tired of managing it on an everyday basis. He hired one manager, then another, but neither handled the agency and its varied personalities properly. Ayer hired his son-in-law, Wilfred W. Fry, in 1909. Fry had married Ayer's oldest daughter, Anna Gilman Ayer, in 1904. Fry, a hard worker, was made a partner two years later. Ayer gave him the responsibility of managing the agency when the second manager resigned.

During World War I, the agency participated in war-work activities, and Ayer himself donated his energy to the Young Men's Christian Association (YMCA), which provided funding to Europe in its time of need. Rhandeena, his wife, had died in 1914; Ayer, alone, needed something other than the agency to occupy his time.

After the war, businesses spent millions of dollars on advertising, and the agency's profits soared to $500,000 plus in 1919, the year the agency celebrated its 50th anniversary. Francis Wayland Ayer was congratulated for his untiring, ethical approach to advertising by such dignitaries as William Howard Taft, the former president of the United States. The same year Ayer married Martha Lawson.

Four years later Ayer died; he was 75.

In describing F. W. Ayer, George P. Rowell wrote,

He is an indomitable worker; thinks of work all the time, eats little, drinks nothing but water; has no vices, small or large, unless overwork is a vice; is the picture of health; and I sometimes think a good deal such a man as Oliver Cromwell would have been had Oliver been permitted to become an advertising agent.[20]

NOTES

1. Robert L. Heilbroner and Aaron Singer, *The Economic Transformation of America: 1600 to the Present*, 2d ed. (New York: Harcourt Brace Jovanovich, 1984), p. 74.

2. Lewis E. Atherton, "The Pioneer Merchant in Mid-America," *University of Missouri Studies*, Vol. 14 (April 1939), pp. 121–125.

3. Evelyn H. Knowlton, *Pepperell's Progress* (Cambridge: Harvard University Press, 1948), pp. 73–77.

4. George Rogers Taylor, *The Transportation Revolution, 1815–1860* (New York: Holt, Rinehart and Winston, 1951), pp. 174–175.

5. Ralph M. Hower, *The History of an Advertising Agency: N. W. Ayer and Son at Work, 1869–1949* (Cambridge: Harvard University Press, 1949), pp. 13–19.

6. *M'Elroy's Philadelphia Directory* (1842), p. 1.

7. *V. B. Palmer's Business-Men's Almanac* (New York: V. B. Palmer, 1850).

8. Donald R. Holland, "The Adman Nobody Knows: The Story of Volney Palmer, the Nation's First Agency Man," *Advertising Age* (April 23, 1973), p. 108.

9. S. M. Pettengill, "Reminiscences of the Advertising Business," *Printers' Ink* (December 24, 1890), p. 687.

10. Robert G. Albion, *The Rise of New York Port* (New York: Charles Scribner's Sons, 1939), p. 386.

11. George P. Rowell, *Forty Years an Advertising Agent: 1865–1905* (New York: Printers' Ink, 1906), p. 148.

12. Ibid., p. 245.

13. *American Newspaper Reporter* (November 20, 1871).

14. Rowell, *Forty Years an Advertising Agent*, p. 240.

15. Ibid., p. 355.

16. Ibid., p. 454.

17. Folder (advertisement) for N. W. Ayer and Son (April 1880).

18. "Our Creed," Folder (advertisement) for N. W. Ayer and Son (1887).

19. N. W. Ayer and Son announcements (1903, 1905, 1910, 1911).

20. Rowell, *Forty Years an Advertising Agent*, p. 443.

3

How P. T. Barnum Helped
Change the Course of Advertising

INTRODUCTION

In 1910 some celebrated the 100th anniversary of P. T. Barnum.
The same year a writer for *Printers' Ink* mentioned this celebration and proceeded to dismiss Barnum and his contributions to
advertising. According to the writer:

It is entirely misleading to celebrate the "advertising ability" of a man
like Barnum without making some very sharp distinctions. It is as if
medical men should celebrate a hoodoo medicine man of long ago—it
is interesting as a starting point of a profession, but lamentably gross
and misrepresentative of the modern development of it.[1]

However, Frank Rowsome, Jr., claimed that Phineas Taylor
Barnum was "one of a little group of men whose ideas and enterprise permanently shaped the art" of advertising before his
death in 1891.[2]

The purpose of this chapter is to examine Barnum's life and
his contributions to advertising by focusing on his promotional
efforts, to determine which of these two writers is correct in his
assessment of Barnum's role in advertising.

The last section ("Cases of Bad Luck?") focuses on the various
fires that haunted Barnum throughout his professional life.

EARLY YEARS

Phineas Taylor Barnum learned the value of money early in life. For instance, when he was 12, he sold lottery tickets for his grandfather. At 15, he clerked in his father's store. Two years later he opened a porterhouse in Brooklyn; one year later he worked as a bartender in another porterhouse in New York. From the money he earned, he opened a store in Bethel, Connecticut. As Barnum wrote in his autobiography, he learned quickly about consumer behavior. "It was 'dog eat dog'—'tit for tat.' "

Our cottons were sold for wool, our wool and cotton for silk and linen; in fact nearly everything was different from what it was represented. The customers cheated us in their fabrics: we cheated the customers with our goods. Each party expected to be cheated, if it was possible. Our eyes, and not our ears, had to be our masters. We must believe little that we saw, and less that we heard.[3]

One of the first items he advertised was the best-selling lottery ticket. These advertisements consisted of handbills, circulars, gold signs, and colored posters. The language was extravagant, and many of the advertisements rhymed.[4]

When he was 21, he edited and published the *Herald of Freedom* in Danbury, Connecticut, and libeled a deacon of a church, for which he was jailed. Barnum claimed that the deacon had "been guilty of taking usury of an orphan boy." Barnum used the occasion to his advantage, however. When he was released, he rode in a parade that was preceded by a brass band and 40 horsemen and followed by carriages filled with friends and supporters. This event was reported by the press, including Barnum's newspaper:

P. T. Barnum and the band of music took their seats in a coach drawn by six horses, which had been prepared for the occasion. The coach was preceded by forty horsemen, and a marshal, bearing the national standard. Immediately in the rear of the coach was the carriage of the Orator and the President of the day, followed by the Committee of Arrangements and sixty carriages of citizens, which joined in escorting the editor to his home in Bethel.

When the procession commenced its march amidst the roar of cannon, three cheers were given by several hundred citizens who did not join in the procession. The band of music continued to play a variety of national airs until their arrival in Bethel (a distance of three miles), when they struck up the beautiful and appropriate tune of "Home, Sweet Home!" After giving three hearty cheers, the procession returned to Danbury. The utmost harmony and unanimity of feeling prevailed throughout the day, and we are happy to add that no accident occurred to mar the festivities of the occasion.[5]

Three years later he and his wife, Charity Hallett, whom he had married in 1829, moved to New York, where he purchased an interest in a grocery. Barnum learned about Joice Heth, an African American who had been the slave of George Washington's father. She was reportedly 161 years of age. Barnum purchased Heth for $1,000. Through handbills, posters, and advertisements in newspapers the public learned that she was the first to clothe George Washington. Within the first week of her appearance, Barnum earned a profit. After New York, Barnum brought Heth to other cities.

To sell Heth's appearances he placed informative advertisements in newspapers and mailed anonymous letters to editors denouncing her credibility. She is "a humbug, a deception cleverly made of India rubber, whalebone, and hidden springs," he wrote.[6] Receipts and, consequently, profits increased until her death five or six months later. Barnum learned after her death that she had been about 80 years of age. He, like the public, had been deceived.

For the next several years, Barnum earned a meager living. In 1841 he tried to support a family of four by writing advertisements for the Bowry Amphitheater for four dollars a week. According to M. R. Werner, "Barnum was one of the first men in the United States to realize the power of the paid adjective in advertising theatrical attractions."[7]

Later the same year Barnum acquired Sudder's American Museum, which was filled with natural and unnatural curiosities. The museum brought Barnum fame and fortune. He entertained the public with educated dogs, industrious fleas, jugglers, ventriloquists, Gypsies, albinos, giants, dwarfs, rope-dancers, mechanical figures, glassblowers, and American Indians. More important, he knew how to advertise the museum. He placed newspaper advertisements to announce acts; sometimes these advertisements had qualities of incantations:

VISION OF THE HOURIS
VISION OF THE HOURIS
VISION OF THE HOURIS
A Tableau of 850 Men
Women and Children
CLAD IN SUITS OF SILVER ARMOUR
CLAD IN SUITS OF SILVER ARMOUR
CLAD IN SUITS OF SILVER ARMOUR[8]

Other advertisements appeared, but in other forms. A brass band, which could be heard for several city blocks, played harmoniously on the balcony of the museum. Gaslights, which had the effect of modern electronic spectaculars, were placed on top of the museum and illuminated lower Broadway. Large paintings of rare animals were made in panels and placed on the outside of the museum. Banners announcing a rare find were strung across streets. Handbills were used, as well as the reliable news column, which he had perfected. As Barnum wrote:

I thoroughly understood the art of advertising, not merely by means of printers' ink, which I have always used freely, and to which I confess myself so much indebted for my success, but by turning every possible circumstance to my account. It was my monomania to make the Museum the town wonder and town talk. I often seized upon an opportunity by instinct, even before I had a very definite conception as to how it should be used, and it seemed, somehow, to mature itself and serve my purpose.[9]

When ordinary forms of advertising failed, Barnum improvised. For instance, Barnum instructed a man to place bricks on the corners of several streets. Barnum then instructed him to carry at least one brick to each corner and exchange it for the other. The man was not to comment to anyone. On the hour, he was to go to the museum and present a ticket, then enter. Within the first hour, approximately 500 men and women stood and watched, trying to solve the mystery. When the man went to the museum, they followed and purchased tickets, hoping to learn the answer inside. Barnum's walking advertisement attracted so many people that after a few days the police asked Barnum to withdraw the man from the street. Reporters wrote about the event for several weeks. Harvey W. Root wrote, "This was his aim in advertising, the goal for which he strove in all his publicity, to make people 'talk,' to make them wonder 'what Barnum would do next,' and to have the papers repeat and spread it."[10]

Another example of improvisation was his invention of "Dr. Griffin" and his preserved mermaid. "Dr. Griffin" was actually Levi Lyman, an associate of Barnum's. In order to sell the mermaid to the public, Barnum placed stories in numerous newspapers. These stories informed readers that Dr. Griffin had purchased the mermaid in China for the Lyceum of Natural History in London but that he would be exhibiting the specimen at Concert Hall for one week. A week later Barnum announced that he had secured the rare specimen for the American Museum. According to Frank Presbrey, "Barnum told the public that the 'Wonder of Creation' had been viewed at Concert Hall by 'hundreds of naturalists and other scientific gentlemen' who 'beheld it with real wonder and amusement.'"[11] Because of the advanced publicity, the exhibition was a success; the museum's receipts more than doubled the first week—from $1,272 to $3,341.93.

Another example of improvisation occurred when he hired a man to accuse the American Museum with swindling him out of 25¢. The man had paid 25¢ to see the "bearded woman" at the museum. The man believed the woman was actually a man garbed in a dress "to deceive and defraud" the public. The man asked that Barnum be punished. The trial was covered by the press, which Barnum had desired. Barnum protested his innocence. For additional publicity, Barnum recruited witnesses who testified to the gender of the "Bearded Lady." These witnesses included her father, her husband, and several physicians who had examined her. An editor of a Connecticut newspaper observed:

[B]eing a case of so novel a character, the newsmongers caught it up and reported it at great length, giving our friend Barnum the advantage not only of a most extensive free advertisement of the Bearded Lady still on exhibition at the Museum, but in a form which his money could not well have purchased.[12]

The publicity was so arranged "that the newspaper accounts of the trial and the sworn evidence of the Bearded Lady's genuineness would appear just at the right time to attract business to the museum on a national holiday."[13]

In addition to these uncommon forms of publicity, Barnum implemented baby shows, baby contests, and beauty contests to arouse the public's curiosity. He was undoubtedly the first in the United States to use these shows and contests to attract attention. He was responsible for implementing the first successful advertising campaigns. He realized that campaigns increased sales. According to Frank Rowsome, Jr.:

In Barnum's time advertising was simply a series of announcements, a process but not a progression. His acute sense of timing told him that this was wrong, that any promotion should have a carefully timed sequence, leading up to a crescendo of interlocked advertising and publicity.[14]

He applied this belief in advertising "Tom Thumb."

MIDDLE YEARS: "TOM THUMB"

Charles Stratton, a midget, was born in Connecticut. When he was five, his parents signed an agreement with Barnum that allowed Barnum to exploit the child; the parents could accompany their son and would get paid. However, for the first year, the family earned only $7 a week, plus food and lodging. When the receipts increased after the first year, Barnum raised their income to $25 a week. In order to sell "Tom Thumb," Barnum had him tour the United States. Barnum advertised the age of "Tom Thumb" as 11 instead of 5. He advertised his place of birth as England instead of Connecticut. He had "Tom Thumb" introduced to prominent families, which was mentioned in advertisements. Biographies as well as lithographs were printed and distributed wherever he toured. Newspaper editors published stories about him, which sparked additional interest. When he appeared at the American Museum most of the public had read about him and desired to see him. Barnum introduced him as "General Tom Thumb freshly arrived from England," and the crowds laughed. In the 13 months he was at the American Museum, almost 100,000 persons paid to see him.

Barnum, who had grown to enjoy the General, brought him to Europe, where they entertained royalty, including the duke of Wellington and Queen Victoria. Dressed like Napoleon, Tom Thumb made an unforgettable impression on the noble class. He and Barnum were invited to rambling palaces and plush estates and chateaus. News stories featured these exploits primarily because readers desired to learn about society's elite.

Barnum had a miniature carriage built for the General:

It was a four-wheeler, with a body eleven inches wide and twenty high, painted red, white and blue. The door handles, hub caps and lamp brackets were silver. The plate-glass windows had Venetian blinds. The cushions were covered with yellow silk. The panels of the doors displayed Britannia and the Goddess of Liberty, supported by the British lion and the American eagle, with the motto, "Go Ahead!"[15]

The carriage cost Barnum $1,500. Barnum purchased four Shetland ponies to pull the carriage and hired an eight-year-old as the coachman and a seven-year-old as the footman. Both were garbed in tailored attire. Wherever the carriage with Tom appeared, crowds cheered.

In Paris the General was so popular that a café was named Tom Ponce. Artists begged him to sit for them. Composers wrote songs about him. Shop windows displayed statuettes of him.

After Paris, they toured southern France, Spain, Belgium, and other European countries. General Tom Thumb was greeted with the same enthusiasm wherever he toured. Barnum applied reverse psychology in his advertising. Before the General appeared anywhere, Barnum had an announcement posted. He directed the public not to get excited but to keep quiet. As he wrote, "Strange as it may seem, people who were told to keep quiet would get terribly excited, and when the General arrived excitement would be at fever heat . . . and the treasury filled!"[16] The tour lasted three years. Approximately 5 million persons paid to see Tom Thumb. He had been kissed by four queens and thousands of other women. The tour's profits were more than $1 million; Tom Thumb's share was half. Barnum was not greedy, and Tom Thumb toured in one of Barnum's shows for several years. They remained friends for life.

MIDDLE YEARS: JENNY LIND

Jenny Lind was the most famous performer in Europe. According to Ruth Hume, "She had everything: a thrilling voice, dramatic talent, and a reputation for piety, modesty, and good works."[17] Barnum had read about her when he was touring Europe with General Tom Thumb, and he desired that she tour America. He hired an Englishman to offer her $1,000 per concert, plus expenses. Jenny accepted with stipulations. Barnum had to assure her that he would hire her conductor, composer, and pianist, as well as a 60-member orchestra. He also had to deposit in a London bank $187,500 before she left Europe.

Barnum soon realized that most Americans had not heard of Jenny Lind. Therefore, he had to enlighten them. An excerpt from his first press release set the tone:

Miss Lind has numerous better offers than the one she has accepted from me; but she has great anxiety to visit America. She speaks of this country and its institutions in the highest terms of praise, and as money is by no means the greatest inducement that can be laid before her, she is determined to visit us.

In her engagement with me (which includes Havana as well as the United States) she expressly reserves for herself the right to sing for and give charitable concerts whenever she may think proper.

Since her debut in England, she has given to the poor from her own private purse more than the whole amount which I engaged to give her, and the proceeds of concerts for charitable purposes in Great Britain, where she has sung gratuitously, have realized more than ten times that amount. During her last eight months she has been singing entirely for charitable purposes, and is now founding a benevolent institution in Stockholm, her native city, at a cost of $350,000.

A visit from such a woman, who regards her high artistic powers as a gift from heaven, for the melioration of affliction and distress, and whose every thought and deed is philanthropy, I feel persuaded, will prove a blessing to America, as it has to every country she has visited, and I feel every confidence that my countrymen and women will join me heartily in saying, "God Bless Her!"[18]

Barnum then distributed an authorized biographical pamphlet and photograph that informed the reader of her inimitable talent.

Before Jenny left for the United States, she gave two concerts in Liverpool, at Barnum's request. Both sold out. A critic in London covered the concerts, then wrote a review that praised her performances. When the review appeared in one of the newspapers hours later, several copies were sent to Barnum. The review, which detailed "the unbridled enthusiasm of the Liverpool audience and its grief at Jenny's imminent departure,"[19] was published in newspapers throughout the United States before she arrived.

Barnum then wrote a letter addressed to himself. The letter, which was supposed to be from Julius Benedict, her composer, appeared in the *New York Daily Tribune*:

I have just heard Mlle. Jenny Lind, whose voice has acquired—*if that were possible*—even additional powers and effect by a timely and well-chosen repose. You may depend on it, that such a performance as hers—in the finest pieces of her *repertoire*—must warrant an unprecedented excitement. . . . Mlle. Lind is very anxious to give a Welcome to America in a kind of national song, which, if I can obtain the poetry of one of your first-rate literary men, I shall set to music, and which she will sing in addition to the pieces originally fixed upon.[20]

The letter was followed by an announcement about a song-writing contest. To enter, one had to write a poem that could be set to music. Barnum received more than 700 entries. The winner, poet Bayard Taylor, received $200.

When the ship entered New York harbor, Barnum, together with a reporter from the *New York Tribune*, greeted it. When the ship docked on Sunday, September 1, 1850, about 40,000 persons were present. They followed her and her entourage as they traveled in Barnum's carriage to the Irving House Hotel. Barnum, surveying the crowd, realized that his promotional efforts had paid off. Hume wrote, "New York merchants eagerly abetted Barnum's grand design by rushing into print to advertise hastily renamed Jenny Lind products: everything from Jenny Lind cigars to Jenny Lind sewing stands, gloves, scarves, riding hats, and perfume."[21]

Barnum then promoted the Great Jenny Lind Opening Concert Ticket Auction. He persuaded his friend John Genin to be the first person in the United States to purchase a ticket to hear Jenny sing. Barnum then visited Dr. Brandreth, who was known for his patent medicines, and persuaded him to purchase the first ticket at auction. Barnum assured him that it would be an excellent opportunity for him to advertise his medicines. When the auction occurred, several thousand were present to bid against one another, including Genin's bookkeeper and Dr. Brandreth's cashier. The cashier's bid of $25 was the first. Genin's bookkeeper bid $50. Others announced various bids. However, everyone, except Genin's bookkeeper, stopped bidding at $225.[22]

The publicity was so encouraging that Barnum repeated the auction in several cities. The reviews of her performances were filled with superlatives; some critics claimed that she was the greatest singer they had heard. Barnum, of course, was ecstatic. Although he was wealthy, he realized that such publicity would help sell tickets and consequently add to his fortune.

The tour covered more than 15 cities in the United States and Canada, as well as Havana, Cuba. Jenny gave more than 90 concerts, not the 150 that had been planned. Barnum claimed that he renegotiated Jenny's contract after her successful performances at Castle Garden in New York. The renegotiation benefited Jenny, not Barnum, as she was provided a percentage of profits in addition to her fee. Barnum claimed that the renegotiation was his idea, not Jenny's.[23]

On June 9, 1851, Jenny informed Barnum she was ending the tour. Barnum and Jenny parted friends. The tour he had managed earned more than $700,000. Others in her entourage encouraged her to leave Barnum and tour alone. Jenny tried, but she was not very successful. Organizing the advertising was too difficult. Her affection for Otto Goldschmidt, her pianist, was blossoming; they were married on February 5, 1852, in Boston.

On May 24, 1852, she performed her last concert in the United States in Castle Garden, the concert hall where she had performed her first.

The campaign for Jenny Lind was characteristic of Barnum's brilliance. "It converted her, in the months before her arrival in this country, from a relatively unknown soprano to the toast of America, greeted by ecstatic thousands who vied to draw her carriage."[24]

LATER YEARS: JUMBO

Years later, when Barnum was a proprietor of a circus, he propositioned his leading competitor, James A. Bailey, and together they merged "The Greatest Show on Earth" with the "London Circus." Barnum knew that the circus needed a major attraction. Jumbo, the largest elephant in captivity, was in the London Zoo. Barnum offered $10,000 for the animal. The superintendent agreed. Reporters in London learned of the agreement and interviewed statesmen and others, who urged that the sale be canceled. The following excerpt appeared in the *London Daily Telegraph* and reflects the sentiment of the British press at the time:

Our amiable monster must dwell in a tent, take part in the routine of a circus, and, instead of his by-gone friendly trots with British girls and boys, and perpetual luncheon on buns and oranges, must amuse a Yankee mob, and put up with peanuts and waffles.[25]

The press in the United States, on the other hand, encouraged Barnum to go through with the purchase.

The sale was finalized, and Jumbo was brought to the United States. When the ship entered New York harbor, Barnum was present. Thousands of spectators waited patiently for Jumbo to be brought ashore. Jumbo was hauled to Madison Square Garden, as thousands lined the streets. Public interest was widespread. Although Barnum had paid $10,000 for Jumbo and $20,000 for the elephant's transportation to the United States, he grossed more than $30,000 the first week the elephant was on display.[26]

Newspapers carried stories about Jumbo, and readers sent hundreds of gifts. Consumer products were named for, or compared to, Jumbo's strength or size. When the Brooklyn Bridge was completed, Jumbo tested its strength. Thousands lined the shores to watch.

On September 15, 1885, after "The Greatest Show on Earth" had performed in St. Thomas, Ontario, Jumbo and a smaller elephant were led to a train car. The trainer saw an unexpected freight train approaching and tried to get both elephants off the track; the engineer saw the elephants and applied the brakes. Jumbo was hit and killed; the smaller elephant was injured. Barnum informed the press that Jumbo had pushed the smaller elephant to safety, and the news was cabled all over the world. Millions, like Barnum, were deeply saddened. Never missing an opportunity, Barnum the showman arranged for Henry Ward, the nation's leading taxidermist, to prepare Jumbo for exhibition.

Eventually, Jumbo was given to Tufts University. A fire destroyed the hide in 1975. The skeleton was donated later to the American Museum of Natural History.

From the campaigns discussed, it is easy to summarize Barnum's philosophy of advertising: first, he realized that one needed to keep one's name or business before the public; second, he realized that unique or original devices could be used to produce conversation as well as attention; third, he realized that one needed to take advantage of every opportunity to bring about editorial comment or news; and fourth, he realized that one needed to provide more real value than one's competition. Barnum's success, reputation, and number of imitators proved that he was correct not to use the more traditional methods of advertising of his day but the unusual methods of advertising that he perfected. Thus, the writer for *Printers' Ink* apparently overlooked the above, which undoubtedly had a dramatic influence on advertising.

Barnum, like advertisers today, advertised primarily to generate interest and, consequently, income.

CASES OF BAD LUCK?

In 1846 Barnum employed carpenters and other laborers to construct a Chinese- and Turkish-style, lavish mansion along the sea in Fairfield, Connecticut. Two years later he moved his family to Iranistan, his new home, where he remained until his financial support of the Jerome Clock Company, which ultimately went bankrupt, forced him to leave Iranistan in 1856. Barnum retreated with his family to a rented house in New York. Iranistan was closed and boarded.

In 1857 Barnum, who was desiring to return to Iranistan until it was sold or auctioned, hired carpenters and painters to repair it. Apparently, one of the worker's pipes, which had been carelessly misplaced, set fire to the mansion, and it burned to the ground. Barnum was in New York. He received a telegram about the fire from his brother, Philo. Although the home was worth $150,000, it was insured for only $28,000. Of course, the mansion would have been sold, and Barnum would have lost it anyway.

In 1865 Barnum became a member of the legislature of Connecticut and was speaking to the body July 13, 1865, when a telegram from his son-in-law, S. H. Hurd, was handed to him. The telegram informed him that his famous American Museum in New York was burning. Barnum continued his oratory. The following morning he went to New York to see what remained of his museum. Later, he wrote,

Here were destroyed, almost in a breath, the accumulated results of many years of incessant toil, my own and my predecessors', in gathering from every quarter of the globe myriads of curious productions of nature and art—an assemblage of rarities which a half million of dollars could not restore, and a quarter of a century could not collect.[27]

A reporter for the *New York Times* wrote that the fire began in the engine room:

The fire originated in a defective furnace in the collar under Groor's restaurant, beneath the office of the Museum, at No. 8 Ann-street, and was first discovered by an employee of the Museum, at precisely thirty-five minutes past noon.[28]

The following day a reporter for the *New York Times* wrote that the origin of the fire was a mystery: "Some of the employees of the Museum were notified a day or two ago that threats of burning the establishment had been made, but little attention was paid to this information."[29]

Although the cause of the fire was never learned, an employee, H. O. Tiffany, claimed that he discovered flames on the second, third, and top floors, which, of course, suggests that one or more persons were responsible for the fire.

Undeterred by his loss, which he estimated to be $400,000, Barnum opened Barnum's New American Museum on November 13, 1865. However, it, too, burned on March 3, 1868. According to a reporter for the *New York Times*:

At 12:30 o'clock Broadway was startled by the cry of "fire!" and flames were seen issuing from the south window on the third floor of No. 539 Broadway. . . . The fire was burning on the third floor, and the interior was only dimly lighted by the flames. The escape of smoke was slight, leaving the impression that there was very little of it, or that it was crowding down into the lower stories.[30]

The next day a reporter for the *New York Times* wrote:

The conflagration is claimed to have been the result of a defective flue, which on the third floor set fire to the cages of some birds that pressed against it. These were made of light, inflammable wood in the first instance, and had been made dry as tinder by long contact with the flue. The fire was first discovered from the street, and during its early stages burned exclusively at the south window of No. 537, as stated yesterday, showing that it had originated in the extreme front of the building.[31]

Barnum was asleep at his home in New York; he learned about the fire the next morning when he read the newspaper. Barnum claimed he lost more than $250,000 as a result of the fire.

In 1872 the Hippotheatron, a multisided wood-and-iron building in New York, which Barnum purchased for his Grand Traveling Museum, Menagerie, Caravan and Circus, burned, killing most of the animals. A writer for the *New York Times* wrote:

At 4:10 o'clock yesterday morning, as Patrolman Raymond, of the Fifteenth Precinct Police, was on duty on Fourth-avenue, near Fourteenth-street, his attention was attracted by cries of "Fire." He ran down Four-

teenth-street toward Third avenue, and when he arrived opposite Barnum's Museum he found volumes of smoke issuing from the building.[32]

Later, the reporter wrote, "The origin of the fire has not yet
been definitely ascertained, but it appeared most probable that
it was caused by the heating apparatus in the back part of the
building."[33]

In the next day's *New York Times*, a reporter wrote:

Fire-Marshal McSpedon stated to a *Times* reporter that he had no doubt
that the fire had originated from the steam-pipes leading from the
boiler-room through the flooring. When the place was examined by the
Fire-Marshal attention was called to the fact that the pipes were in too
close proximity to the flooring boards. This defect was partially reme-
died, and the flooring cut away, but one of the wooden beams was
allowed to rest against the main steam-pipe leading from the boiler, and
it was this beam that probably took fire and communicated the flames
to the rest of the building.[34]

In the December 29 issue of the *New York Times*, a reporter
presented Fire Marshal McSpedon's report concerning the fire.
McSpedon reiterated his initial beliefs about the fire's origina-
tion, as the following excerpt illustrates:

In my opinion, as an expert, the fire originated under the floor, immediately over the boiler, and from superheated steam, which in its effects
is as destructive as burning gas or flame, and where it is allowed to
gain strength is sure to be the cause of terrible results.[35]

In 1887 Barnum and Bailey's Winter Quarters in Bridgeport,
Connecticut, which contained numerous buildings that housed
numerous animals, caught fire. The fire, which started in the
main building for animals at 10:00 P.M., not only killed most of
the animals but burned every building. A reporter for the *New
York Times* wrote, "The fire started in the horse room." The reporter added:

The watchman making his rounds discovered the fire and started to
give the alarm, when some unknown person hit him on the head with
a blunt instrument, felling him to the ground and cutting a number of

severe gashes on his head. He staggered to his feet and gave the alarm, enabling the other watchmen in the building, who were preparing for bed, to escape.[36]

In the November 22, 1887, issue of the *New York Times*, a reporter wrote:

George W. Myers, the watchman who discovered the fire and sounded the first alarm, had an experience that seems to prove the fire to have been of incendiary origin. He found the door of the stable in which the ponies were housed open when it ought to have been closed. The stable was already on fire. He sounded the alarm, then laid the lantern he was carrying on the ground, and was about to enter the stable to loose the ponies when he was struck on the head with a billy by an unknown man. He lay unconscious, he supposes, for 10 or 15 minutes. When he recovered the fire was raging in all quarters of the main building, which was about 200 feet broad by 500 feet long.[37]

In the same story, Barnum was asked about the fire; his response was lengthy. Barnum claimed that the fire was a blessing in disguise, at least to the public. He added: "Besides, it will give us a lot of free advertising. That, of course, will be some compensation for our loss." Later, he informed the reporter that a greater show would rise from the ashes. Barnum said, "I begin to think it was a good thing we were burned out after all."[38]

Barnum revealed that the land in Bridgeport, on which the Winter Quarters had been constructed, had increased in value, and, consequently, he would not rebuild the Winter Quarters on it.

The reporter ended the story with the following:

Sunday's fire was the seventh from which the old showman has been a direct sufferer. In October, 1852, his showy residence in Bridgeport, known as Iranistan was nearly destroyed by fire. Five years later the same house, reconstructed and refurnished, was completely destroyed, entailing a loss of about $125,000. In July, 1865, the American Museum, at Broadway and Ann-street, was burned, and in March, 1868, his new museum on Broadway, near Prince-street, was completely wiped out by fire. Three years later, December, 1871, the Hippotheatron was totally destroyed by fire, and in July, 1873, fire burned up a tent and all its furnishings while the show was in Chicago. Taken altogether, Mr. Barnum's losses will aggregate close to $1,000,000.[39]

What is troubling about these fires is that none seemed to bother Barnum. His reactions, which he described in his autobiography, displayed unconcern, even when at least two of the fires may have been started by arsonists. Although he lost money as a result of each fire, financially he rebounded quite successfully, as a result of the publicity about each fire. Certain individuals called Barnum "the arsonist." Of course, this accusation was made in haste and was not based on any evidence. However, fires followed Barnum throughout his professional life.

Barnum made enemies. It is not inconceivable to think that one or more of his enemies may have been responsible for one or more of the fires. For instance, he and James Gordon Bennett, the publisher of the *New York Herald*, had several confrontations, including a major dispute over real estate. When Barnum's Museum burned in 1865, Barnum, who held the lease for the property, realized the property's value. According to Barnum:

The next day I met Mr. James Gordon Bennett, who told me that he desired to buy my lease, and at the same time to purchase the fee of the Museum property, for the erection thereon of a publication building for the *New York Herald*. I said I thought it was very fitting the *Herald* should be the successor of the Museum; and Mr. Bennett asked my price.[40]

Barnum sold the lease for $200,000 to Bennett. According to Barnum, Bennett had agreed to purchase the property for $500,000. "He had been informed that the property was worth some $350,000 to $400,000, and he did not mind paying $100,000 extra for the purpose of carrying out his plans."[41] However, the parties who estimated the value of the property were not aware of the lease, which, of course, would have decreased their estimate by $200,000. Barnum wrote,

When . . . Mr. Bennett saw it stated in the newspapers that the sum which he had paid for a piece of land measuring only fifty-six by one hundred feet was more than was ever before paid in any city in the world for a tract of that size, he discovered the serious oversight which he had made; and the owner of the property was immediately informed that Bennett would not take it.[42]

Next, Bennett had his lawyer speak to Barnum in an effort to persuade him to take back the lease and return the $200,000, but Barnum refused. Eventually, Bennett, who had signed an agreement to purchase the property from the owner, was sued by the owner. Before the suit was tried, however, Bennett purchased the property for the agreed amount. Needless to say, Bennett never forgot Barnum. Whether Bennett was responsible for one of the fires is debatable.

NOTES

1. "Barnum and Advertising," *Printers' Ink* (July 14, 1910), p. 193.

2. Frank Rowsome, Jr., *They Laughed When I Sat Down: An Informal History of Advertising in Words and Pictures* (New York: McGraw-Hill Book Co., 1959), p. 29.

3. M. R. Werner, *Barnum* (New York: Harcourt, Brace and Co., 1923), p. 15.

4. Frank Presbrey, *The History and Development of Advertising* (New York: Doubleday, 1929), p. 212.

5. *The Herald of Freedom*, December 12, 1832.

6. Rowsome, *They Laughed When I Sat Down*, p. 30.

7. Werner, *Barnum*, p. 42.

8. E. S. Turner, *The Shocking History of Advertising* (New York: E. P. Dutton & Co., 1953), p. 130.

9. P. T. Barnum, *Barnum's Own Story: The Autobiography of P. T. Barnum* (New York: Dover Publications, 1961), p. 102.

10. Harvey W. Root, *The Unknown Barnum* (New York: Harper and Brothers, 1927), pp. 205–206.

11. Presbrey, *The History and Development of Advertising*, p. 216.

12. Root, *The Unknown Barnum*, p. 208.

13. Ibid., p. 209.

14. Rowsome, *They Laughed When I Sat Down*, p. 30.

15. J. Bryan III, *The World's Greatest Showman: The Life of P. T. Barnum* (New York: Random House, 1956), p. 56.

16. Ibid., p. 59.

17. Ruth Hume, "Selling the Swedish Nightingale: Jenny Lind and P. T. Barnum," *American Heritage* (October 1977), p. 99.

18. *New York Commercial Advertiser*, February 29, 1850.

19. Hume, "Selling the Swedish Nightingale," p. 103.
20. *New York Daily Tribune*, August 14, 1850.
21. Hume, "Selling the Swedish Nightingale," p. 104.
22. Ibid.
23. P. T. Barnum, *Struggles and Triumphs or, Forty Years' Recollections of P. T. Barnum* (New York: Macmillan Co., 1930), pp. 204–205.
24. Rowsome, *They Laughed When I Sat Down*, p. 30.
25. Theodore James, Jr., "World Went Mad When Mighty Jumbo Came to America," *Smithsonian* (May 1982), p. 138.
26. Ibid., p. 146.
27. Barnum, *Barnum's Own Story*, p. 363.
28. "Barnum's American Museum Burns," *New York Times*, July 14, 1865.
29. "The Late Fire," *New York Times*, July 15, 1865.
30. "Burning of Barnum's Museum," *New York Times*, March 3, 1868.
31. "Burning of Barnum's Museum," *New York Times*, March 4, 1868.
32. "New-York Fires," *New York Times*, December 25, 1872.
33. Ibid.
34. "The Museum Fire," *New York Times*, December 26, 1872.
35. "The Recent Fires," *New York Times*, December 29, 1872.
36. "A Great Loss to Barnum," *New York Times*, November 21, 1887.
37. "Barnum on Top as Usual," *New York Times*, November 22, 1887.
38. Ibid.
39. Ibid.
40. Barnum, *Struggles and Triumphs*, pp. 489–490.
41. Ibid., p. 490.
42. Ibid.

4

Advertising Patent Medicine: The Rise of Lydia Pinkham

INTRODUCTION

Those who lived in the colonies depended on homemade remedies to cure illnesses. Usually, the formulas for these remedies were passed from one generation to another. Or colonists could visit physicians, who would charge them for their Indian-type remedies; however, many colonists could not afford physicians. Or they could purchase patent medicines, which, in most cases, caused drunkenness.

Advertisements for patent medicines appeared in newspapers during the 1700s and 1800s, partly because advertising paid the bills. Many newspapers, especially colonial newspapers, would have died after a few issues had it not been for these advertisements.

In the 1720s and 1730s, for instance, vaccination against smallpox was discussed in newspapers. Most of this discussion was in advertisements created primarily to sell cures. Most of these advertisements were written in a straightforward style. By 1736, creativity had replaced the straightforward style of copy, as the following advertisement for Dr. Bateman's Pectoral Drops, which appeared in the *Pennsylvania Gazette*, July 1, 1736, illustrates:

Dr. Bateman's PECTORAL DROPS, which are given with such great Success in all Fluxes, Spitting of Blood, Consumptions, Small Pox, Measles, Colds, Coughs, and Pains in the Limbs or Joints; they cure Agues, and the most violent Fever in the World, if taken in Time, and give present Ease in the most racking Torment of the Gout; the same in all sorts of Pains (be they ever so violent) they give Ease in a few Minutes after taken; they ease After-Pains, prevent Miscarriages, and are wonderful in the Stone and Gravel in the Kidneys, Bladder and Ureters; bringing away Slime, Gravel, and oftentimes Stones of a great bigness, and are the best of Medicines for all Stoppages or Pains in the Stomach, Shortness of Breath, and Straitness of the Breast, re-enkindling the almost extinguish'd natural Heat in diseas'd Bodies, by which Means they restore the languishing to perfect Health: Their manner of working is by moderate Sweat and Urine. For Children's Distempers, no Medicine yet discover'd can compare with it: For it cures the Gripes in their Stomach and Bowels, by expelling Wind upwards and downwards. It causes weak and forward Children to take their natural Rest.

It is taken with great Success in the Rickets, and, in a Word, it hath, restored Hundreds of poor Infants to their strength and liveliness, that have been reduced to meer Skeletons.

Sold by *Miles Strickland* in *Market-Street, Philadelphia*, price 3 s. a Bottle, with Directions.[1]

This remedy, according to the advertising, cured more than 30 illnesses, diseases, or abnormalities. Only three shillings a bottle, the product sold well throughout the century. Other imported patent medicines were also advertised throughout the colonies, and most, like Dr. Bateman's Pectoral Drops, offered the consumer relief from practically any illness or disease.

As newspapers increased in size and in number of pages, more medicines were advertised. Some advertisers mentioned that their concoctions were sanctioned by royalty. For instance, in the February 19, 1770, issue of the *Boston Chronicle*, the London Book-Store of Boston advertised the Essence of Pepper-Mint, by His Majesty's Royal Letters Patent.[2] The product sold for one shilling four pence. In return, the consumer received "speedy relief" from colic, gout, and other illnesses.

During and after the Revolutionary War, advertisements for imported medicines were curtailed. Americans realized that the need for medicines was great. Consequently, Americans started advertising what they produced. Lists of medicines sold at apothecaries were advertised weekly. Physicians also served as dentists, veterinarians, druggists, and barbers and often advertised their services and cure-all potions.

In the 1800s, advertising for patent medicines occupied most of the space in numerous newspapers. Products such as Dr. Ryan's Incomparable Worm-Destroying Sugar-Plums, Turlington's Balsam of Life, Godfrey's Cordial, Steer's Genuine Opodeldor, Stoughton's Bitters or Elixir, Antipertussis, Lockyer's Pills, James' Fever Powder, Dalbey's Carminative, and Anderson's Pills, just to name a few, were advertised from New England to Florida. It seemed that certain names and labels could ward off illnesses, even if the product could not.

Mineral waters, such as Dr. Willard's Mineral Water, Ballston or Congress Mineral Water, and Godwin's Celebrated German Water, were advertised like patent medicines; that is, the copy was filled with outrageous claims. For instance, in a mineral water advertisement that appeared in the June 15, 1803, issue of the *New York Herald*, Dr. Willard claimed that the water from his mineral spring in Connecticut could cure such maladies as "Erisipelas, Salt Rheum, Leprous Affections, and indeed almost every cutaneous complaint," including cancer, gout, paralytic disorders, and other diseases.[3]

In the 1830s and 1840s, certain patent medicines romanticized the American Indian through illustration, name, and advertising copy. For instance, Dr. Freeman's Indian Specific not only used the word to identify his product but persuasively pointed out that his product was produced from herbs that Indians used to cure consumption. Wright's Indian Vegetable Pills, which sold exceptionally well in the 1840s, were advertised as "THE ORIGINAL AND ONLY GENUINE INDIAN MEDICINE."[4]

Makers of patent medicines soon realized that it was more profitable to manufacture and advertise several remedies for several illnesses instead of producing one remedy and advertising it as a cure-all. Dr. Bardwell, for instance, had Aromatic Lozenges of Steel, Re-Animating Solar Tincture or Pabulum of Life, Genuine Ague and Fever Drops, and Annodyne Essence—all for different illnesses. Other companies, like Michael Lee and Company of Baltimore, marketed numerous patent medicines.

Some companies manufactured gadgets that were to be worn. Supposedly using electricity, these devices were said to restore the nervous system as well as cure all kinds of diseases. Of course, the advertisements were false. These gadgets could not cure illnesses. Yet, like advertisements for patent medicines, the advertisements for these contraptions were filled with superlatives. Words or phrases such as "genuine," "original," or "nature's own" were used often. Testimonies, too, were used.

By the end of the 1800s the nation's households were filled with patent medicines and devices. Both died in the early 1900s because newspapers were receiving advertisements from other manufacturers and businesses and because muckraking journalists discredited the patent medicine industry and consequently encouraged lawmakers to enact certain legislation that would eliminate or at least restrict its availability.

This chapter examines Lydia E. Pinkham and her Lydia E. Pinkham's Vegetable Compound, one of the most popular patent medicines of its day, as well as the journalistic campaign against patent medicines.

LYDIA E. PINKHAM AND HER VEGETABLE COMPOUND

Lydia Pinkham, who was born on February 9, 1819, in Lynn, Massachusetts, to William and Rebecca Estes, was responsible for concocting a vegetable compound that was targeted primarily to women before the 1900s. She was the tenth of a dozen children.

Pinkham's father, a shoemaker turned farmer and owner of real estate, provided his family with physical comfort. Her mother introduced the family to the controversial ideas of Emanuel Swedenborg, a Swedish scientist and theologian who claimed to have experienced a spiritual world where people went after they died. Followers of Swedenborg were abolitionists. They were vegetarians, too, and abstained from drinking alcohol. Pinkham herself was undoubtedly influenced by Swedenborg's ideas. For instance, she joined the Lynn Female Anti-Slavery Society when she was 16.

Pinkham graduated from the Lynn Academy. She taught school and in 1843 met Isaac Pinkham, 29, a widower with a young daughter. They married later the same year. Remaining in Lynn, Pinkham gave birth to Charles Hacker Pinkham in 1844 and Daniel Rogers Pinkham a year later. Daniel died, however, in 1847. Pinkham gave birth to more children over the years. Isaac Pinkham, a dreamer, worked at numerous jobs and often spent more than he earned. In 1857 he moved the family to Bedford, Massachusetts, and tried farming. Three years later the family returned to Lynn. Although the family earned a meager living during the years of the Civil War, Isaac's investments in land eventually brought the family some financial security. In 1873, however, certain banks failed, and others, including those in Lynn, threatened to foreclose on mortgages. Isaac was sued and almost arrested for not being able to pay his debts; as a result, his health deteriorated.

The family struggled but survived. Lydia, who had added ingredients to a formula that had been given to her husband as part of a settlement on a debt, had been brewing a medicine that supposedly cured "women's weakness." Lydia allowed members of her family and friends to test the formula. Apparently, the formula worked; "women's weakness" declined. However, Lydia did not think of advertising and selling the product. That thought occurred to Daniel, one of her sons, and Lydia E. Pinkham's Vegetable Compound was begun in 1875. The four-page pamphlet *Guide for Women* was distributed, and the product, which contained 19 percent alcohol, was brewed in the cellar and bottled.

The Lydia E. Pinkham Medicine Company, with Will Pinkham, another son, as proprietor, primarily because he had no outstanding debts, officially organized in 1876, and Daniel and Will traveled to various towns and cities to market the product. Eventually, druggists, who had been successful stocking other patent medicines, began ordering the Vegetable Compound. However, sales of the medicine were minuscule, particularly in cities such as Brooklyn, where Daniel tried several forms of advertising in addition to distributing the pamphlet. He also suggested that the advertising copy in the pamphlet include other parts of the anatomy, such as the kidneys, besides the uterus.

Later, he placed the pamphlet's contents as an advertisement in the *Boston Herald*, for which he was criticized by his family because the advertisement was too expensive. However, the ad-

vertisement proved somewhat successful, and the family hired
T. C. Evans to create advertisements for newspapers.

In 1879 Daniel thought of adding a photograph of a woman
to the advertisements. The woman, he realized, needed to appear
healthy and trustworthy. Daniel knew immediately that his
mother's face displayed the motherly, if not grandmotherly, image he had imagined. After much discussion, she agreed to pose
for the photograph that graced the product's labels and countless
advertisements.

After her face graciously adorned advertisements for a year,
sales of the product dramatically increased, and the family was
offered six figures for the company and its appealing trademark;
the family refused the offer.

In 1881, after battling tuberculosis for two years, Daniel died;
he was 32. Will, who was also ill with lung disease, died the
same year; he was 28. Lydia was stricken with grief; in 1882 she
suffered a stroke, then died several months later, in 1883. She
was 64.

The company continued to prosper, nonetheless, under the
family's guidance, and Lydia Pinkham's face continued to appear on labels and in advertisements. The following advertisement, for instance, appeared May 3, 1887, in the *New York
Times*:

LYDIA E. PINKHAM'S
VEGETABLE
COMPOUND

Offers the
SUREST REMEDY
For the
PAINFUL ILLS AND DISORDERS SUFFERED BY WOMEN
EVERYWHERE.

It relieves pain, promotes a regular and healthy recurrence of periods
and is a great help to young girls and to women past maturity. It
strengthens the back and the pelvic organs, bringing relief and comfort
to tired women who stand all day in home, shop and factory.

Leucorrhea, Inflammation, Ulceration and Displacements of the
Uterus have been cured by it, as women everywhere gratefully testify.
Regular physicians often prescribe it.

Sold by all Druggists. Price $1.00.
Mrs. Pinkham's "Guide to Health" mailed to any lady sending stamp
to the Laboratory, Lynn, Mass.[5]

A line drawing of Lydia E. Pinkham was positioned to the left
of the headline. Her pen, which had advised countless female customers about
their health, continued to answer inquiries. Other advertisements
for the compound contained scientific information that was discussed in medical books, such as Dr. Frederick Hollick's *The Origin of Life* and Dr. John King's *The American Dispensatory*, which
Pinkham had read, and focused on numerous medical conditions, including leukorrhea and dyspepsia. Over the years other
maladies were added to the list for which the compound was
the perfect remedy. The advertising copy discussed symptoms
that most individuals, especially women, experienced. Thus, to
a certain extent, the advertisements manipulated readers into
thinking they were ill. As a result, they were persuaded to try
the compound. Other advertisements contained testimonials reportedly from customers whose illnesses had been cured by the
compound. The Lydia E. Pinkham Medicine Company, of
course, desired for women to use the compound, not see physicians, who were not necessarily well educated. Besides, most
physicians were men, and the company's literature, including
advertisements, contained an antimale bias.

The advertising was now created by Harlan Page Hubbard,
who purchased space at very low rates and sold it to the Lydia
E. Pinkham Medicine Company at very high rates. Eventually,
the family learned of Hubbard's exorbitant charges and decreased the advertising budget. Sales dropped. In 1890 the family
hired another agent and limited his commission. The advertising
budget was increased; sales soared for at least several years, and
the company earned a sizable profit.[6]

In 1899, however, sales declined for the first time in 9 years,
probably as a result of the company's slashing its advertising
budget earlier the same year. During the next 10 years sales continued to decline, no matter how much the advertising budget
was increased.

THE JOURNALISTIC CAMPAIGN AGAINST
PATENT MEDICINES

One explanation for the decline in sales was Cyrus Curtis, publisher of *The Ladies' Home Journal* and *Collier's Weekly*, who stopped accepting advertising for patent medicines in 1892. A second explanation was Edward Bok, editor of *The Ladies' Home Journal*, who wrote lengthy editorials against the patent medicine industry in the early 1900s. For instance, "The 'Patent-Medicine' Curse" disclosed the amount of alcohol in different brands; "Why 'Patent Medicines' Are Dangerous" revealed that manufacturers of patent medicines were not obligated by law to list all ingredients on labels; and "A Diabolical 'Patent-Medicine' Story" disclosed the questionable marketing efforts for two patent medicines.

Bok hired Mark Sullivan to investigate Dr. Ray Vaughn Pierce and his product, Dr. Pierce's Favorite Prescription, primarily because Dr. Pierce had brought suit against *The Ladies' Home Journal* for libel. Bok had claimed that Dr. Pierce's product contained alcohol, opium, and digitalis. Dr. Pierce proved that his product did not contain opium or digitalis by having the product chemically analyzed.

Sullivan failed to find any evidence against Dr. Pierce or his product, and Bok lost the suit. However, Sullivan's investigation into patent medicines continued, and his investigative article about the patent medicine industry, specifically the Proprietary Association, "The Patent Medicine Conspiracy against Freedom of the Press," was published in *Collier's Weekly* in 1905. Sullivan was also responsible for informing the public that Lydia E. Pinkham had died in 1883 and was buried in Pine Grove Cemetery in Lynn, Massachusetts.

Samuel Hopkins Adams, another investigator of the patent medicine industry, contributed several in-depth articles under the main title "The Great American Fraud" to *Collier's Weekly* in 1905. He revealed the amount of alcohol found in various patent medicines and claimed that women were in a constant stupor. He revealed the chemical formula for Liquozone in another article and discussed the exaggerated claims and false testimonials for the product in another article. Other articles about other questionable patent medicines followed.

Later, editors and writers of *Collier's Weekly* and *The Ladies' Home Journal* advocated federal regulation to control or prohibit patent medicines from being sold. Such regulation had been discussed by certain members in Congress for some time. Members of the American Medical Association, however, were divided. Certain members realized that a pure food and drug law could conceivably curtail sales of certain products by restricting advertising and possibly prohibit the manufacture of other products. Nonetheless, the Pure Food and Drug Act was signed in the summer of 1906 and took effect the first day of 1907. As a result, all medicines that crossed state lines had to meet certain standards of purity and had to print accurate information on the packages and labels. Lydia E. Pinkham's Vegetable Compound was no exception. For the first time, the company was forced to reveal the amount of alcohol and to delete the exaggerated claims from the package and label. However, the Lydia E. Pinkham Medicine Company, like other makers of patent medicines, realized that it was the responsibility of the consumer to notice the changes on the package and label. The company also realized that advertisements could imply what its advertisements had claimed, and the implications would be almost as effective as the claims had been. The company's advertising agent, James T. Wetherald, placed reading notices in various newspapers primarily to convince readers that the Pure Food and Drug Act eliminated dangerous drugs from the market. Wetherald emphasized that the Lydia E. Pinkham's Vegetable Compound was safe and healthy and de-emphasized the amount of alcohol, which was almost 20 percent. As a result of his efforts, sales increased over the years. In 1912, for instance, sales were above $1 million.

OTHER PROBLEMS

Critics of patent medicines were still writing articles and books, and Arthur J. Cramp, of the American Medical Association's Department of Propaganda, notified the Internal Revenue

Service that because of Lydia E. Pinkham's Vegetable Compound's alcoholic content the product should be taxed. The Internal Revenue Service informed the Lydia E. Pinkham Medicine Company that the product's formula had to be changed or the product would be taxed; the company complied and changed the formula, which was finally accepted by the Treasury Department in 1914. However, the product's taste was not the same, and sales decreased during the next several years.

The company faced federal litigation in 1915, when a complaint concerning the product's effectiveness was filed. The company's lawyers claimed that the chemical analysis on which the complaint was based was for the old formula, and therefore the complaint was out of date. Eventually, the company was fined $50, primarily for false claims that had appeared on labels. The company paid the fine and changed the labels.

In 1919, with the passage of the Volstead Act, the company feared that the government would classify the product as an alcoholic beverage. Although the company thought of decreasing the amount of alcohol, the change was never made. In 1925, based on chemical analysis, the government pressured the company to stop marketing the product as a medicine exclusively for women. Later the same year the company complied and changed the labels and advertisements.

In 1926 Lydia Pinkham Gove was determined to pit herself and her mother, Aroline Gove, against the Pinkham side of the family for control of the company. Arthur Pinkham was now president of the company, but the Goves controlled the finances. Lydia battled Pinkham, even though the company's board of directors had given him absolute control of the company's operations. However, when Wetherald died, Lydia created an advertising agency primarily for the purpose of saving the company money and concurrently played a role in the company's direction. Although several family members, including Charles Pinkham, confronted Lydia, she persevered by not supporting any advertising that had not met with her approval.

Eventually, the matter was brought before the courts when the Pinkhams initiated legal action in 1936. The court sided with the Pinhams in the sense that the Goves were not to interfere in the business. Lydia, undeterred, refused to obey the court, and another suit was filed. Lydia had her day in court and lost. The judge sided with the Pinkhams.

In 1938 the Federal Food, Drug, and Cosmetic Act was passed. This legislation required patent medicines to list the ingredients on their labels. The same year the Federal Trade Commission cited the company for its advertising. According to the Federal Trade Commission, the advertising exaggerated the product's benefits to women. The company used outdated medical research to support the claims of its advertising and lobbied the Federal Trade Commission, which allowed the product to be advertised as being helpful to women.

The company conducted an advertising campaign that addressed various female problems, and sales increased. In 1945, for instance, sales passed $2.5 million. The Food and Drug Administration, on the other hand, demanded medical evidence from the company that supported the claims made in the advertisements. The company conducted extensive research and claimed that the product indeed alleviated certain female symptoms. Although the Food and Drug Administration did not file a complaint against the company, it nonetheless scrutinized the company's advertising.

Sales of the product decreased dramatically in 1950. The American woman had changed, and the product was viewed as a pseudoremedy from the previous century. Lydia E. Pinkham, dressed in clothes designed for the 1900s, was replaced by a modern, attractive female character. However, sales continued to decrease. The company hired a research firm to conduct a market analysis in the late 1950s. The firm's report suggested that the company change the product and its advertising. Apparently, the newly fashioned character did not appeal to the modern American woman.

Although the company attempted another advertising campaign, sales sagged. In 1968 the company was sold to Cooper Laboratories, a pharmaceutical company. Cooper Laboratories moved the facility to Puerto Rico to cut production and import costs. Unfortunately, Cooper Laboratories could not save the product. Lydia E. Pinkham's Vegetable Compound became a product that few female consumers purchased.[7]

NOTES

1. *Pennsylvania Gazette*, July 1, 1736.
2. *Boston Chronicle*, February 19, 1770.
3. *New York Herald*, June 15, 1803.
4. Cedric Larson, "Patent-Medicine Advertising and the Early American Press," *Journalism Quarterly*, Vol. 14, No. 4 (December 1937), p. 338.
5. *New York Times*, May 3, 1887, p. 2.
6. Stephen Fox, *The Mirror Makers: A History of American Advertising and Its Creators* (New York: William Morrow and Co., 1984), pp. 18–19.
7. Sarah Stage, *Female Complaints: Lydia Pinkham and the Business of Women's Medicine* (New York: W. W. Norton and Co., 1979).

5

John Wanamaker and His Influence on Retail Advertising

INTRODUCTION

In the 1800s, primarily as a result of the Industrial Revolution, there "emerged a vast culture of consumption."[1] According to William R. Leach, "Advertising gave it shape; a new abundance of commodities established its foundation."[2] This culture emphasized service as well as competition and depended on the imagination of owners and/or operators of various businesses to promote the goods that they stocked.

The department store, unlike the small, cramped dry goods shop of an earlier period, exemplified this culture. Department stores had appeared after the Civil War in major cities throughout the United States. By the late 1800s, these stores occupied as much space as a city block and contained several stories, each of which was filled with numerous commodities for the prospective customer to examine. Numerous large department stores held street fairs and carnivals as well as tied promotional efforts to certain holidays or other days.

These department stores also emphasized decorations such as Egyptian temples, French salons, and Japanese gardens. Concurrently, these stores employed various colors and glass to highlight certain departments and/or commodities. The latter was also employed for displaying jewelry. Light, too, was employed for specific effects. The sales appeal of some products, for instance, was enhanced by light.

The department stores' show windows became a major instrument of promotion. People walking on sidewalks were invariably attracted to what was displayed in the stores' windows. In the early 1900s, windows became ministages in the sense that they were used as props to highlight one or two products.

In the early 1900s, the larger department stores often had zoos, restaurants, botanical gardens, beauty and barber shops, museums, fairs, post offices, and libraries, among other attractions and departments, to attract people's interest.

In addition, these large emporiums sold countless personal products as well as numerous commodities for the home. However, Leach wrote that department stores

did not simply "sell" commodities: they intervened with advertising skills to amplify the excitement of possibility inherent in the commodity form. They attempted to endow the goods with transformative messages and associations that the goods did not objectively possess.[3]

By advertising, using displays, and stocking particular brands of goods, the large department stores made people, especially women, fashion-conscious. As women became important consumers of department store merchandise, owners and/or operators hired women as assistant managers and sales clerks. After all, they reasoned, women knew what women needed or desired.

One of the most successful owners of a large department store was John Wanamaker. He had learned about the American consumer a century before Sam Walton opened his first Wal-Mart store.

JOHN WANAMAKER

John Wanamaker was born on July 11, 1838, to Elizabeth Kochensperger and Nelson Wanamaker near Philadelphia. His parents, Protestants, were devout Christians. His father was of German and Scottish descent, and his mother was of French Huguenot descent.

Wanamaker learned about money from his father, who, with

his father, John, operated a brickyard. Wanamaker "turned" bricks before and after school, for which his father paid him seven copper cents. However, in 1849, because of competition, Wanamaker's grandfather retired from the brickyard and moved to a farm in Indiana. Wanamaker moved with his parents to the farm in 1850. Farming undoubtedly was hard work. The family experienced a harsh, bitter, cold winter, and Wanamaker's grandfather died. Wanamaker's mother, whose family and friends lived in Philadelphia, grew homesick. Wanamaker's father realized that the family needed a change. Besides, farming had not been that productive.

Wanamaker, like his father, missed his grandfather very much. He said: "My grandfather was a pioneer. I attended his funeral in Indiana. I will not in my lifetime forget the inscription on his gravestone, reading my own name on it. Standing at the grave, I prayed that I might become as good a man as he was."[4]

Nelson Wanamaker moved his family to Philadelphia, where he returned to making bricks. Wanamaker attended school until he was almost 14 years of age. Then he was employed as an errand boy by Troutman and Hayes, publishers of various reference books, for which he was paid $1.25 a week.

In 1852 Wanamaker was hired by Barclay Lippincott, a clothing store, at a salary of $2.50 a week. Although his salary eventually doubled, his tasks were menial at best. Wanamaker grew frustrated; he desired to have the opportunity to employ his ideas about advertising and selling. Eventually, he was hired by Colonel Bennett, who owned the largest clothing store in Philadelphia, Tower Hall. Wanamaker was paid $6 a week. More important, he was granted the opportunity to apply what he knew and what he gradually learned, even though he was only 16 years of age.

At first, Wanamaker polished the large knobs on the front door. Then he learned the stock and subsequently became a proud salesman. Always energetic, he was promoted; he was put in charge of the men's clothing department and persuaded Colonel Bennett to allow him to purchase certain items such as shirts and socks for the department. Wanamaker learned to buy and save the store money. However, in 1857, as various businesses failed because of the economy, his health deteriorated. Tall and thin, he worked long hours at the store, then devoted hours to religious activities at the First Independent Church. He was advised by a physician to leave Philadelphia and rest.

Years later, Colonel Bennett was asked about John Wanamaker. He replied, John was certainly the most ambitious boy I ever saw. I used to take him to lunch with me, and he would tell me how he was going to be a great merchant. He was always organizing something. He seemed to be a natural born organizer. This faculty is largely accountable for his great success in after-life.[5]

At 19 years of age, Wanamaker traveled to the Northwest, where his health improved. After several months, he journeyed east, to Philadelphia, where he contemplated studying for the ministry. His pastor, Dr. John Chambers, had been an inspiration to him. Wanamaker realized that he did not have the formal education to become a minister, so he became involved in the Philadelphia Young Men's Christian Association (YMCA), which had been founded by George Stuart in 1854. Wanamaker was hired as a full-time secretary of the organization in 1858; he earned $1,000 a year. However, he was responsible for asking members to increase their contributions, which, as he soon learned, was not an easy task. Certain members criticized him and the organization, and pastors of churches resented their members' giving contributions to the YMCA and not to their churches. Nonetheless, he persevered and recruited 2,000 new members in his first year as secretary. He was responsible for the organization's engaging in evangelistic programs as well as instrumental in the organization's efforts to help the army during the Civil War. He was also responsible for raising money to purchase the building in which the organization was located. He remained active in the organization until 1887.

Wanamaker's first love, however, was Bethany Church and Sunday school, which he founded three years before Oak Hall and two years before he married Mary Brown. He was proud of Bethany Church, and because of his religious convictions, he devoted considerable energy and money to its development and growth.

In 1861 Wanamaker approached Colonel Bennett about purchasing an interest in Tower Hall. Bennett, who respected Wanamaker and his abilities, refused Wanamaker's proposition. Wanamaker approached his brother-in-law, Nathan Brown, and proposed that they open a men's clothing store. Although family members and several friends attempted to discourage them, Wanamaker and Brown opened Oak Hall on April 8, 1861. Sales totaled $24.76 the first day. Wanamaker desired to stock merchandise that would have an immediate appeal. He traveled to New York to purchase goods on credit. When these goods were displayed in the store, the first advertisement appeared in the *Public Ledger* on April 27, 1861:

OAK HALL CLOTHING BAZAAR
Southeast corner Sixth & Market Streets

WANAMAKER & BROWN desire to say to their many friends and the public generally, that they open to-day with an entire new and complete stock of ready-made clothing; and having purchased their goods under the pressure of the times at very low rates, will sell them accordingly.[6]

Other brief advertisements for Wanamaker and Brown were scattered in the same column as this advertisement and were headed "Oak Hall Clothing Bazaar," "Whole Suits for Three Dollars," "Right at the Corner," "John R. Houghton," and "Opens To-day." John R. Houghton, the store's cutter, encouraged his friends to visit the store.

The price for the suits attracted attention. However, profits from sales were not high, and advertising was comparatively expensive. During the first few months, the proprietors earned very little. Occasionally, even money for their lunches went to pay for advertising. According to Linda Kowall, "Store advertisements were generally simple notices of goods for sale, printed in microscopic type and buried inside the newspapers."[7]

Wanamaker, who had tried to serve his country but was turned down because of his health, secured contracts to clothe the officers of two regiments. This experience encouraged him to secure similar contracts for police officers, firemen, and military cadets months later.

Wanamaker, now a father of a son, enjoyed retailing, even though the business demanded most of his attention. His wife seldom saw him during the day but nonetheless listened to his ideas at night. Mary, always supportive, enjoyed being married to a young entrepreneur.

One of the store's first policies was to guarantee certain fabrics such as all-wool, which attracted new customers. Advertising quality goods helped establish Wanamaker and Brown as a reputable clothier. Wanamaker realized that price, too, had to be advertised in order to appeal to certain prospective customers. However, problems in marketing were evident; sales suffered periodically. Wanamaker finally realized that the solution or at least part of the solution to lagging sales may be found by studying the consumer. To him, merchandising should be a public service, not an argument between the retailer and the customer over price. Thus, in addition to guaranteeing the quality of the goods in his store, Wanamaker ticketed every article. Although he was given credit for initiating the one-price system in retail merchandising, he claimed that A. T. Stewart, who owned a large department store in New York, was the first to employ the one-price rule for dry goods. In 1865 the firm announced that customers could return an article and get their money back, as long as the article had not been used. The policy of "money back" was revolutionary in the sense that it had not been used by any merchant; it was also revolutionary for Wanamaker and Brown's sales, which increased dramatically.

In addition to advertising in newspapers, Wanamaker employed outdoor advertising. He hired painters to paint "W. & B." in letters 12 feet high on boards all over Philadelphia. He had handbills distributed at county fairs. He used large balloons to attract attention to his store, as well as toy balloons, which were given to children. Other instruments that were used to announce Wanamaker and Brown included Oak Hall slates, pencils, tracing books, children's books, picture postcards, pen-and-ink sketches, calendars, clocks, and the cover as well as inside pages of the 1865 *City Directory*.

Nathan Brown, his partner, died in 1868, the year Wanamaker and Brown became the largest retailer of men's clothing in the country. Wanamaker purchased his partner's interest in the business and established John Wanamaker and Company in 1869 on Chestnut Street, which, to a certain extent, resembled the store owned by A. T. Stewart of New York. Wanamaker's new store was luxurious; it contained a skylight in the center, which was open; carpeting; paintings; and mirrors. Wanamaker stocked lines of clothing that would not have sold in Oak Hall. He desired to attract a different clientele that preferred service and quality rather than price.

The store had six departments by 1874. These included gentlemen's ready-made clothing, youths' and boys' ready-made clothing, a children's department, ladies' coats and habits, "bespoke" and measure goods, and a haberdashery.

The same year he placed the first half-page advertisement that was ever published in a newspaper, even though he depended, to a certain extent, on the store's windows to attract potential shoppers. However, the advertising for the Chestnut Street store was more restrained than the advertising for Oak Hall.

Although Mary had given birth to more children, the third son, Horace, had died in infancy, and the oldest daughter, Hattie, died when she was five years of age. The Wanamakers had four children who were bringing them considerable happiness, however. The Wanamakers also traveled, but most trips abroad were for the purpose of purchasing goods for the stores.

Wanamaker opened additional stores in other cities but soon realized that these stores were not managed according to his wishes. As a result, he closed various branch stores and concentrated on those in Philadelphia.

In 1876 he opened the largest department store of its kind. Termed the Grand Depot, Wanamaker's "New Kind of Store" had been the Pennsylvania freight depot. Wanamaker had paid almost $500,000 for the land and the structure. This sum did not include the costs for renovation. The Grand Depot was devoted to clothing, including men's. Wanamaker advertised the store's opening with fanfare, attempting to attract visitors who had come to Philadelphia for the Centennial Exhibition. Inside the store, "the spruced-up shed counters radiated outward in concentric circles, their arcs broken by aisles that criss-crossed the shed like grand avenues. Wanamaker embellished the facade with minarets and a Moroccan motif."[8]

Wanamaker focused on high volume and low cost, a focus that was extremely profitable, and to prevent sluggish sales periods he advertised special sales, which, for the most part, moved goods. He wrote many of the advertisements for the store. Although display advertisements had become common, his advertisements, even when they were large, were filled with conversational language that discussed the bargains of the day.

According to Leach, "Wanamaker claimed that his 'New Kind of Store,' as he put it, was built principally for profit but also in response to the needs of the people."[9]

In 1877 the Grand Depot offered additional lines of clothing, including women's. The emporium was termed a "dry goods store" by George W. Childs of the *Public Ledger*, as Wanamaker purchased additional lines of goods and added new departments. The Grand Depot's success was staggering. The number of employees increased from more than 600 to more than 1,200 within a year. Wanamaker introduced shoppers to electrical lighting in 1878. Electricity also helped him solve the problem of ventilation.

Wanamaker also published several journals that contained anecdotes, comments, and advice about shopping. These journals included *Everybody's Journal*, which was published first for Oak Hall shoppers and employees, then for the general public at a cost of 10¢. *The Farm Journal*, which was published for the first time in 1879 for the Grand Depot, also attained respectability among the public. In 1879 *The Ladies' Journal*, which contained poems and articles, was targeted to women. In addition to these journals for the stores, Wanamaker published several religious periodicals for his church.

Wanamaker placed the first full-page newspaper advertisement of any retail merchant in 1879. Linda Kowall noted that

This new "Wanamaker Style" of advertising—the bold use of consecutive full-page advertisements which were like news items themselves—marked the beginning of his unprecedented effort to make a science of advertising. To create advertisements . . . Wanamaker began to educate his advertising staff, sending them to visit factories, interview artists and become familiar with quality, sources of supply and manufacturing processes. In addition to its impact on modern advertising practices, the Wanamaker Style, soon emulated by other retailers, played a major role in the rapid rise of powerful and increasingly independent city daily newspapers by infusing them with the advertising dollars, which began to provide a substantial and reliable new revenue base.[10]

In 1880 John E. Powers, who had written advertisements for the Lord and Taylor department store in New York, was hired by Wanamaker to create advertisements that were honest, direct, and simple. Powers employed a typeface that was much more readable than other typefaces found in advertisements, and his advertisements were undeniably attractive. However, Powers was independent and, to a certain extent, not open to suggestions, even suggestions by Wanamaker. His closed-mindedness and candor forced Wanamaker to dismiss him in 1886.

By 1881 Wanamaker's Grand Depot had almost three acres of selling space on one floor, 46 departments, and more than 2,000 employees. Wanamaker had pneumatic tubes installed between the sales clerks and the cashier's office; as a result, cash transactions took less time. Other physical improvements, such as steam heating, carpeting, artwork, and music, occurred over the years, which made the Grand Depot one of the public's favorite places to shop. For instance, according to Neil Harris, "Wanamaker . . . filled his stores with pictures, careful to select and hang them to maximum effect. He objected to the crowding of pictures in museums, which he likened to a three-ring circus."[11]

Wanamaker was the first American retailer to place buyers of merchandise in various European cities. Wanamaker, who had hired his friend Robert Curtis Ogden to manage Oak Hall in 1879, invited Ogden to help him manage the Grand Depot. His oldest son was also involved in the management of the Grand Depot. Wanamaker's brothers managed the Chestnut Street store.

In 1886 he introduced the half-day Saturday to his employees. This reduced the workweek to five and a half days. (In 1914 Saturdays in July and August were made full holidays.) He also provided medical benefits and a retirement system for his employees.

In 1887 Wanamaker entered the wholesale dry goods business when he purchased three wholesale businesses, one of which was the third largest in the country. By 1888 his new business was prosperous.

Wanamaker, a Republican, dutifully supported Benjamin Harrison's campaign for president and, as a result, was respectfully asked by Harrison to serve as postmaster general of the United States. Although Wanamaker was criticized by Harrison's advisers, Harrison refused to budge. Wanamaker, after he and Harrison discussed the position, accepted and immediately recommended to Congress that a rural free delivery system be implemented throughout the United States so that every citizen, especially those who lived in the country, would have access to the postal system. Congress allowed Wanamaker to test his idea in small towns, which he attempted to do without much financial support from the government. Later, Wanamaker requested a parcel post service, which was criticized and not implemented until years later. Wanamaker was also criticized for recommending that postal rates for books and newspapers be increased. He also recommended that the government own and operate the telegraph and telephone systems. Owners of certain businesses and companies as well as certain congressmen were happy when Wanamaker left Washington in 1893.

In 1896 Wanamaker established the John Wanamaker Commercial Institute, a school that was for the young boys who worked at his retail stores. The institute was eventually expanded to include girls and older boys who had been deprived of a proper education. (In 1908 the institute was chartered as the American University of Trade and Applied Commerce.)

When Wanamaker returned to Pennsylvania, he waged an unsuccessful battle against M. S. Quay, a politician who had considerable clout. In 1896, for instance, Wanamaker sought the Republican nomination for the U.S. Senate. Two years later, he sought the Republican nomination for governor of Pennsylvania. Both races were controversial primarily because of the questionable nature of the campaigns. Voters learned little from the press about the candidates, especially Wanamaker. Coverage was devoted to character assassination, which Quay's political machine waged. However, Wanamaker was successful in revealing Quay's corrupt practices, and Quay was indicted. Although he was acquitted, his popularity rapidly declined. He lost the election.

Wanamaker entered the New York retail market in 1896, when

he purchased A. T. Stewart and Company. He enlarged the advertising staff and demanded that every writer of advertising copy actually examine articles of clothing before writing a word. Wanamaker's advertisements, which were large and illustrated, appeared every day except Sunday in various daily newspapers. Wanamaker was a firm believer in the power of advertising, especially during periods when sales were off. In an interview with Frank G. Carpenter, he said:

When the times are hard and people are not buying, is the very time that advertising should be the heaviest. You want to get the people in to see what you have to sell, and you must advertise to do that. When the times are good they will come of their own accord. But I believe in advertising all the time. I never stop advertising.[12]

Under the watchful eye of Wanamaker, Robert C. Ogden and his staff maintained the New York store until it, like the other Wanamaker stores, had become successful. Although many had predicted failure because of the store's location, Wanamaker was victorious.

Wanamaker purchased adjoining property and had a 14-story building erected. The building, which was connected to the older building as well as to the recently completed subway system, was designed to display furnishings for the home. For instance, the upper floors were devoted exclusively to furniture, floor coverings, house furnishings, glassware, and draperies. The lower floors contained specialty shops for men. The building also contained the House Palatial, which was a private home consisting of 22 rooms; a large, magnificent restaurant; a three-story, 1,300-seat auditorium; and a storage plant for furs.

The building, which opened in 1907, tripled the selling space of Wanamaker's in New York. Wanamaker used the older building for women's wear and dry goods. When Ogden retired, Wanamaker put his son Rodman in charge of the New York store.

Later in 1907 panic struck the financial center in New York, and Wanamaker's sales began to decrease. Concurrently, he feared that he could not complete the addition to his building in Philadelphia, which had been started, even though he was assured by his friends, including those who were loan officers in banks, that he would be given a loan if he so desired. Wanamaker weathered the financial storm. Unfortunately, certain small creditors requested payment. Wanamaker paid the few who demanded settlements and, primarily because of his deep religious beliefs, endured. Of course, he could have sold his business for millions and walked away, but he was determined to keep the business in his hands.

The same year, as if his financial problems were not enough to worry about, his home outside Philadelphia, Lindenhurst, was destroyed by fire. Wanamaker's loss was estimated to be more than $2 million. Wanamaker built a second Lindenhurst on the same property.

The following year sales were also sluggish, and the doomsayers were predicting failure. Wanamaker, on the other hand, was optimistic. He placed large orders, which helped wholesalers and manufacturers; he completed the building in Philadelphia. The same year his son Thomas B. Wanamaker, who had been ill, died; he was 47. Wanamaker, already burdened with financial problems, was stricken with grief. He focused on his business.

Finally, in 1909, sales increased, which not only helped Wanamaker but silenced the doomsayers. Wanamaker, acknowledging that the business in New York was rebounding, returned to Philadelphia, where a new building was almost ready to open in time for the Golden Jubilee—the celebration of 50 years in business.

In October 1911, more than 6,000 employees and family members helped Wanamaker celebrate 50 years of serving the public. Other luncheons and events sponsored by various organizations were scheduled primarily for the purpose of honoring him.

Now in his early 70s, Wanamaker was advised by some to retire. Others suggested that he let his son Rodman handle the business. However, when he was in Philadelphia, he went to his office every day except Sunday. When he was in New York for any period of time, he maintained the same routine.

Wanamaker, who remained active in politics, voiced his opinion when World War I erupted. He opposed Woodrow Wilson and supported Charles Hughes for president. In time he supported Wilson's position. He even wrote brief, pro-American "editorials" that prefaced his businesses' daily advertisements. These editorials explained how Wanamaker's was helping in the war effort and what the average American citizen thought as he or she learned about certain developments or events. Wanamaker also aided the Red Cross and directed the Liberty Loan campaigns. He devoted considerable time, energy, and money to both causes.

In 1918, at 80 years of age, he served as one of the directors of the War Welfare Council. He continued his patriotic chore until the Treaty of Versailles was signed. After the war, American lives changed. Many were working for the first time. Wages of those who had been working for years suddenly climbed, and the cost of living increased. Prices of goods and services, too, increased, which worried Wanamaker. Could the average American afford to shop at Wanamaker's if prices continued to increase?

In response to this question, Wanamaker decided to offer every product in his stores at 20 percent off the ticketed price. The advertisement that announced this decision appeared on May 3, 1920. On May 8, a Saturday, a world's record was established for the amount of sales in a retail store: Wanamaker's sold more than a million dollars' worth of merchandise. Certain Philadelphia and New York merchants adopted a similar policy. In time the idea spread across the country. Wanamaker ended his sale July 2. The high cost of living actually slowed as a result of Wanamaker's brilliant scheme.

In 1921 he had been in business 60 years. Celebrations occurred in Philadelphia and New York, and Wanamaker was the guest of honor.

On December 12, 1922, he died from heart failure. Financiers and certain retailers attempted to persuade Wanamaker's heirs to sell the business, but the store remained independent for years. For instance, Rodman managed the business until his death in 1928. The company was then managed by trustees for the benefit of Rodman's children. Although the Stewart store closed in 1952, and the store next to it closed two years later, another store was built in New York and remained in the family's control.

In 1978, however, Wanamaker's, which had 16 stores and sales of more than $300 million a year, was purchased by the Carter Hawley Hale Stores, a California-based department store chain. The stores had been acquired by Woodward and Lothrop before Woodward and Lothrop filed for bankruptcy in the mid-1990s.

In summary, in addition to his emphasis on advertising, Wanamaker was the first to offer vacations, with pay, to his employees; the first to introduce electricity and the telephone into a retail business; the first to open reading and resting rooms for his customers; the first to build a hotel for his female employees; the first to provide Christmas bonuses to his sales staffs; the first to build a camp for the boys who worked in his stores; the first to establish Saturdays in July and August as holidays for his employees, with pay; the first to offer medical service to his employees; the first to introduce the satisfaction-guaranteed-or-your-money-back policy; and the first to install an elevator in a retail business, to mention a few firsts.

According to Leach,

He translated the new economy into a new culture for many Americans—we might call him one of this country's domesticators of commercial culture, a man who not only "revolutionized retailing," as he said himself, but who also legitimated fashion, fostered the cult of the new, democratized desire and consumption, and helped produce a commercial environment steeped in pecuniary values.[13]

NOTES

1. William R. Leach, "Transformations in a Culture of Consumption: Women and Department Stores, 1890–1925," *The Journal of American History*, Vol. 71, No. 2 (September 1984), p. 319.

2. Ibid., p. 320.

3. Ibid., p. 327.

4. Herbert Adams Gibbons, *John Wanamaker*, vol. 1 (Port Washington, N.Y.: Kennikat Press, 1971; originally published in 1926), p. 21.

5. Thompson Brown, "Hon. John Wanamaker: From Messenger-Boy to Merchant Prince—A Romance of Business," *Our Day*, Vol. 17, No. 113 (September 1897), p. 404.

6. *Philadelphia Public Ledger*, April 27, 1861, p. 1.

7. Linda Kowall, "Original and Genuine, Unadulterated and Guaranteed!" *Pennsylvania Heritage*, Vol. 15, No. 1 (1989), p. 20.

8. Maury Klein, "John Wanamaker," *American History Illustrated*, Vol. 15, No. 8 (December 1980), pp. 10–11.

9. William Leach, *Land of Desire: Merchants, Power, and the Rise of a New American Culture* (New York: Pantheon Books, 1993), p. 113.

10. Kowall, "Original and Genuine, Unadulterated and Guaranteed!" p. 22.

11. Neil Harris, *Cultural Excursions: Marketing Appetites and Cultural Tastes in Modern America* (Chicago and London: University of Chicago Press, 1990), p. 65.

12. Gibbons, *John Wanamaker*, vol. 2, pp. 25–26.

13. Leach, *Land of Desire*, p. 34.

6

Albert Lasker and the Lord and Thomas Advertising Agency

INTRODUCTION

According to Stephen Fox, "If the early twentieth century in advertising history can be described in a phrase, it would be: The Age of Lasker."[1] Lasker worked at, then owned, the Lord and Thomas advertising agency for more than 40 years.

THE EARLY YEARS

Albert D. Lasker was born on May 1, 1880, in Freiburg, Germany, to parents who were from Galveston, Texas. When Lasker was old enough to travel, his parents returned home.

Lasker's father, who had been born in Germany, moved to the United States when he was 16 and eventually settled in Galveston, where he became a successful businessman and president of several banks. Although he loved his children, he was not demonstrative, and Lasker grew up feeling that he had to prove himself to his father. This sense of insecurity plagued Lasker for most of his life.

In elementary school Lasker was a weak student; he was interested in other things besides school work. He enjoyed earning money. At 12 years of age, for instance, he founded a four-page weekly newspaper, which he wrote, edited, and published. Titled the *Galveston Free Press*, the paper earned a profit of $15 a week for more than a year. The paper contained aphorisms, a column on the theater, anecdotes, announcements, and a column by the editor. The paper also contained advertisements. Lasker sold the space, then created the advertisements for the various merchants.

In high school he edited the school magazine—one of the first in the country—and managed the football team. In addition, he worked as a bookkeeper for his father and as a journalist for the *Galveston Morning News*, for which he covered sports, politics, business, crime, and the theater. Upon his graduation in 1896, he worked full-time for the newspaper. He left the *Morning News* when he turned in a review of a play that he had not seen but knew by heart. The play had not been performed because the Opera House had burned. Lasker realized immediately that he had made a serious mistake. Credibility was important to him. He moved to New Orleans and worked for the *Times-Democrat*. Then he moved to Dallas, where he worked for the *Dallas News*. When he returned to Galveston, his father suggested that he go into advertising. Lasker did not like advertising. He desired to edit and publish a small newspaper in Texas. His father agreed to buy a small newspaper for Lasker on one condition: that he work in advertising for a brief period. Lasker agreed, but he never worked in journalism again.

LORD AND THOMAS

Lasker's father knew D. M. Lord, a partner of the Lord and Thomas advertising agency in Chicago, and asked Lord to give his son a job. Lasker left Texas in 1898; he was 18 years of age.

Lasker was given a salary of $10 a week and within a month lost $500 to a gambler; he did not have $500. He went to see Ambrose L. Thomas, the other partner of the agency, and explained what had happened. According to Lasker:

I had never before sold anything to anybody, but I did a salesmanship job that day. I talked Mr. Thomas into advancing me $500—which was a fortune in those days. He went with me, and we settled with the gambler. Both he and I were sure that the gambler had cheated me, but the gambler had the due bill, and so we settled with him for $500.[2]

Lasker could not leave advertising as he had planned. He owed Thomas too much money. He had lost more than money; he had lost his newspaper. Lasker worked first as an office boy. A year later, when a salesman put in his resignation, Lasker asked Thomas if he could take over the salesman's territory until he found a replacement. Thomas agreed. Lasker worked hard and within several months had proved that he could interest clients. One client, the Wilson Ear Drum Company, had been with the agency for several years. Lasker learned that the company's advertisements were considerably small and that the Common Sense Ear Drums were sold by mail. The agency received a 10 percent commission.

Lasker knew that he could improve the client's sales by improving the advertisements. He went to see George Wilson, the owner of the firm, and said:

Suppose Lord and Thomas could multiply your sales. That would be very good for you, and it would multiply our volume of business with you, because you would spend more money. We will write a new kind of copy for you, but you must pay us fifteen per cent commission on all ads that contain the new copy. If at the end of ninety days the results haven't increased, we'll give you back the money, and your account will still be on a ten per cent basis. But as an earnest that you are interested, you will have to pay me a fee of $500.[3]

George Wilson agreed to Lasker's proposition, and Lasker hired Eugene Katz, a friend, to write copy for several advertisements and had a photograph taken of the firm's artist cupping his ear. He showed "The Deafest Deaf Man You Ever Saw" advertisement to the client, George Wilson, who used it, and sales increased:

You Hear!
When you use
Wilson's Common Sense Ear Drums

The only scientific sound conductors.
Invisible, comfortable, efficient. They
fit in the ear. Doctors recommend
them. Thousands testify to their

perfection and to benefit derived.
Information and book of letters from many users, free
WILSON EAR DRUM CO.
104 Trust Building, Louisville, Ky.[4]

The company had been spending $36,000 a year with Lord and Thomas. Within a year the company spent $240,000. Lord and Thomas earned $36,000 from this account instead of the usual $3,600. Lasker had succeeded. He employed this bargaining technique on several clients. Sometimes it worked; sometimes it failed.

Lasker studied copywriting and wondered what caused some advertisements to work and others to fail. He learned part of the answer several years later.

In 1901 Lasker met Flora Warner. He was 21 years of age, and she was 22. Although he had paid his debt to Thomas and was earning $60 a week, he realized that he could not support two people. He met with Thomas and informed him that he wanted $5,000 a year. Thomas asked if he wanted more, but Lasker refused. He informed Thomas that eventually he desired to become a partner.

Lasker married Flora a year later. Their marriage brought them three children. However, Flora contracted typhoid fever and, later, phlebitis and became a semi-invalid who needed medical attention for most of her life.

Lasker's salary had doubled by 1903, when Lord retired. Lasker purchased Lord's share of the agency and was made a partner. Lasker now had time to concentrate on copy.

In 1904 John E. Kennedy sought a position as a copywriter with the Lord and Thomas advertising agency. He had a note sent to Thomas. In the note he had included the following: "I can tell you what advertising is. I know you don't know. It will mean much to me to have you know what it is and it will mean much to you. If you wish to know what advertising is, send the word 'Yes' down by the bell boy."[5] Kennedy was downstairs in a saloon waiting patiently for a response. Thomas, however, dismissed the note, but Lasker was curious. He met with Kennedy. Kennedy informed Lasker that advertising was "salesmanship in print." Whether Kennedy got this idea from Charles Austin

Bates is anyone's guess. However, Bates had said eight years earlier that "advertisements are printed salesmen."[6] Lasker desired to learn more from Kennedy, so he hired him to write copy. From Kennedy, Lasker learned that consumers needed a reason to buy something. If a reason could be given, and it was sound, consumers would react positively toward the product. To Kennedy, a good advertisement contained a logical explanation as to why the consumer should purchase the product. He knew almost instinctively how to attract the client's consumers. He used language that they understood. His advertisements were distinctive. He used heavy, italic type, underlined words, and capitalized letters in the headlines. Through Kennedy, Lord and Thomas pioneered "reason-why" advertising, which other agencies adopted.

Using this form of advertising, Kennedy and Lasker created a speculative campaign for a firm that manufactured washing machines. The company's most popular advertisement depicted a woman chained to a washtub; the headline read, "Don't be chained to the washtub." Kennedy knew that the advertisement was negative and consequently would not work as well as an advertisement that was positive. He created an advertisement that depicted a woman sitting in a chair, reading a book, and turning effortlessly a handle of a washtub. The headline read, "Let This Machine Do Your Washing Free."[7] Lord and Thomas got the account.

Lasker helped publicize Kennedy's discovery in the agency's house organ, *Judicious Advertising*, and in other publications. As a result, Lord and Thomas acquired more clients until it became one of the largest advertising agencies in the United States. According to a writer for the trade journal *Advertising and Selling*, Kennedy's discovery became "the foundation stone of successful advertising."[8] However, Kennedy owed much to Lasker; after all, he hired him.

Kennedy left Lord and Thomas within two years. According to Lasker, "Kennedy left us, for what reason I do not know, and I went on as best I could with the momentum of what I had learned from him and of what the others had learned. We were also learning lessons from the results we were getting."[9] Years later Lasker praised Kennedy's contributions to advertising:

The history of advertising could never be written without first place in it being given to John E. Kennedy, for every copywriter and every advertiser throughout the length and breadth of this land is today being guided by the principles he laid down.[10]

Lasker was now in charge of editing all copy that was written for clients, even though he did not write any himself. He also introduced ideas, that were used in campaigns.

Thomas died in 1906, and Lasker, together with Charles R. Erwin, purchased Thomas' share of the business. Erwin remained a partner until 1912, when he sold his share of the agency to Lasker.

Claude C. Hopkins, one of the best copywriters of his day, was hired by Lasker in 1908. Hopkins employed Kennedy's style but, unlike Kennedy, who had worked very slowly and methodically, worked exceedingly fast. As he put it, he put in two years' worth of work each year he worked. Lasker paid Hopkins well— more than he had paid Kennedy, which was $75,000 a year. Lasker knew that Hopkins was worth every penny. Hopkins enjoyed visiting clients to see how products were manufactured. He visited Quaker Oats and observed how the company produced rice and wheat cereal, then he changed the name of one of the company's products from Wheat Berries to Puffed Wheat and employed the line "The cereal shot from guns." He created memorable advertisements for Goodyear and various automobiles. He emphasized brand images in his advertisements. He realized the significance of conducting tests, using samples, and researching copy to determine which headline, which subhead, and which sentence of body copy attracted the most attention. Hopkins' advertisements were straightforward and simple, with few, if any, illustrations.

Hopkins enjoyed mail-order advertising, in which he eventually specialized. He employed testing through the use of coupons and samples to numerous campaigns. For another product, he learned what plaque meant. The advertisement played up beautiful teeth and how the consumer could have them. In addition, the advertisement offered a sample of the product. By using coupons and samples, he traced who responded, and this piece of information benefited the client.

Lasker learned a great deal from Hopkins, and vice versa. Lasker was responsible for Americans' purchasing orange juice. Lord and Thomas got the Sunkist Growers, Inc. account, and Lasker learned that citrus growers in California produced so many oranges that they cut orange trees to limit the supply. Lasker, primarily to stop the destruction of the trees, had campaigns created to encourage consumers not only to eat oranges but to drink orange juice. Consumption of the product increased so much that trees were spared.

Lord and Thomas acquired the B. P. Johnson and Company account in 1911. The company manufactured soap products, including Palmolive, which, at the time, enjoyed only modest sales. When Lasker and Hopkins learned that the product was colored green because of two ingredients, palm and olive oil, they realized an opportunity. They would play up its beauty instead of its power to clean. The campaign was tested, and within several years Palmolive was the leading brand.

Another client was the Van Camp Packing Company in Indianapolis. Van Camp manufactured canned foods, including pork and beans. Lasker and Hopkins employed tasting demonstrations, then created advertisements that asked consumers to compare Van Camp's pork and beans to other brands. Consumers reacted positively to the advertisements and purchased Van Camp's. For other Van Camp products, they used the power of suggestion and coupons.

Although Lasker preferred that the agency handle clients that manufactured convenience goods, the agency was successful in handling clients that manufactured automobiles and tires. For each client, Lasker relied on the "reason-why" style of copy. For Goodyear, Hopkins created the phrase "No-Rim-Cut Tires," which informed consumers that Goodyear's straight-side tire, if punctured, would not cut the rim. Each campaign was successful because Hopkins focused on the changes that occurred in the industry.

Lasker made several mistakes, however, in his professional career. For instance, he loaned money to one automobile manufacturer and invested in another. The latter cost him almost $1 million. Perhaps he had been naive; after all, he was not that old. Or perhaps he was merely caught up in the times. Industries were changing or growing, and new products were being produced by the hundreds. Lasker learned quickly from his mistakes.

Lord and Thomas continued to prosper. Billings rose from $3 million in 1906 to $6 million in 1912, when Lasker became sole owner of the agency. The agency now had offices in New York, Toronto, Paris, London, San Francisco, and Los Angeles, and Lasker made sure that each office paid for itself. As Don Belding pointed out, "[H]e demanded maximum results from his men ... and he did not let the agency stray into extracurricular activity and gather a lot of appendages, or barnacles as he called them."[11] In fact, Lasker fired a certain number of employees or "deadwood" about every four years. This may be considered by many as a flaw in his character. Those who produced, like Hopkins, stayed with the agency until they left to pursue other opportunities or retired.

Before he became intrigued with politics in 1918, Lasker had contributed much to advertising. He had been partly responsible for the "salesmanship in print" and "reason-why" styles of copy. He had been partly responsible for "scientific" advertising. He helped train personnel, some of whom moved to other agencies or founded agencies. He promoted ethical principles and was vehemently opposed to questionable or dishonest advertising.

For the next several years, Lasker worked first for the Republican party, then the presidential campaign of Warren G. Harding, and finally for the U.S. Shipping Board, which he directed. Lasker did not like working for the government; in 1923 he returned to Lord and Thomas, which Hopkins had been directing. Lasker immediately learned that the agency was not the largest in the country. This fact bothered him immensely. The agency had lost some clients because of internal problems. Personnel in certain offices argued over which style of advertising to employ. Other agencies, such as J. Walter Thompson, were filling advertisements with colorful art, different typefaces, and borders. Headlines, to Lasker, seemed to play a secondary, instead of a primary, role in these advertisements, and body copy was not necessarily "reason-why." Hopkins had created an art department. Lasker was opposed to having an art department because of costs. Hopkins, who for years had gotten along well with Lasker, suddenly realized that there were too many differences between them. He retired from the agency in 1924 and started a copywriting service. His autobiography, *My Life in Advertising*, was published in 1927.

Lasker hired Ralph Sollitt, who had worked for the Shipping Board. Then he fired every employee in the New York office. In order to make Lord and Thomas the largest agency in the country, he had to take drastic steps. First, he talked at great length to his subordinates; he explained how Lord and Thomas was founded as well as what he had accomplished. In short, he presented his life to them and expressed the style of advertising Lord and Thomas should create. Second, advertisements to attract new clients were created and subsequently published in trade journals. These advertisements were subtle compared to advertisements for other agencies, as the following illustrates:

Is Advertising Read?
Three examples that bring out the answer

THE word *halitosis* lay buried in the widely "read" dictionary of the English language scores of years until set in ordinary type in an advertisement it became a by-word of the millions.

As a result, a product 40 years on the market with moderate sales became a world leader. Bad breath became almost a fashion.

On the other hand, yeast was something merely to make bread with—until Fleischmann advertisements said otherwise.

Now we gain fair skins, robust health, cure ourselves of many of the common ills of mankind, and even look forward hopefully to Eternal Youth because of it.

For centuries women used makeshift hygienic pads. The subject itself was admittedly a forbidden one. A subject no one spoke about, much less wrote about, except in medical practice.

Then came Kotex. A sanitary pad. A product no woman had ever heard about. A product that admitted no definitely descriptive words in headlines to describe it.

Thus to learn what Kotex was intended for, the reader had to go *deep into the text* of the ads. Kotex headlines perforce had to be more or less indirect. No person could get the import of a Kotex ad *without reading virtually every word of the ad itself.*

That women did, everyone who follows advertising knows. Over 80% of the better class of women in America today employ Kotex. The makers of this product would be quick to answer whether or not advertising is read.

Thus Listerine, Fleischmann's Yeast and Kotex—at least three of the most notably successful products of the day—must be regarded as Simon Pure Advertising successes.

All had their basic selling stories, not in the headlines, but in the text of their ads. And readers had to read that text to be "sold." All stand as indisputable answers to the question, "Is Advertising Read?"

If people didn't read ads as carefully as news or feature matter, most of the successful concerns whose names are household words would be virtually unknown to the reading millions.

Men who have made money through advertising know how true that is.[12]

Lasker's style of advertising paid off. The agency captured new accounts in the 1920s. One account was the Kimberly-Clark product Kotex. The product had been on the market for some time, but sales were slow. Lasker instinctively believed that Kotex could be sold successfully to women if the correct strategy was implemented. The agency created factual advertisements, which were eventually accepted by certain magazines. A newspaper campaign was created to inform women that Kotex would be available in plain packages in certain stores. Another campaign was created to inform organizations, including school boards, how girls could be taught feminine hygiene. The campaigns worked, and sales increased dramatically.

In 1924 the agency got another Kimberly-Clark product, Kleenex. Lasker, however, was not as interested in this product as he had been in Kotex, primarily because he believed Kleenex would never replace the handkerchief. Ernst Mahler, the inventor of the product, made Lasker realize the importance of the product when he asked, "A. D., do you enjoy putting germs in your pocket?"[13] Lasker persuaded Mahler to increase the size of the product, and the agency staff created a different size box. The advertisements sold Kleenex as the "handkerchief you can throw away."

Lord and Thomas earned millions from Kimberly-Clark. By the end of the 1920s, however, almost 60 percent of the agency's billings came from the American Tobacco Company account Lucky Strike. As Lasker recalled:

The big cigarette companies had started some time between 1912 and 1923 to make the present type of cigarettes, domestic Virginia and Turkish tobaccos mixed. I think the first two to make it were Camels and Chesterfields. The American Tobacco Company was late in starting. Up to 1923, or even 1925, the American Tobacco Company must have had over fifty brands, and those fifty brands would be pushed and advertised—each with a little appropriation.[14]

Lasker got the Lucky Strike account from George Washington Hill, the son of Percival Hill, the president of the company, and persuaded Hill to invest more money in advertising the Lucky Strike brand. By doing so the agency could conduct a national campaign.

One day Lasker and Flora were eating at the Tip Top Inn. Because Flora had gained weight, she had been advised by her doctor to light a cigarette before each meal. When she lit a cigarette on this occasion, the proprietor informed Lasker that he could not allow a woman to smoke in public because it would offend others. This incident opened Lasker's eyes. Women were treated like second-class citizens. He realized that if he could change the public's attitude toward women's smoking in public, he could capture another target market. Lasker thought of women who lived in Europe; they smoked in public. Lasker thought of women who would capture the public's attention. He recalled:

It was very natural that my mind went to the opera stars, because at that time there were only one or two American stars, and the rest were foreign.
Then we developed what we called our "precious voice" campaign. As they were singers, they said, "My living is dependent on my being able to sing, and I protect my precious voice by smoking Lucky Strike."[15]

The advertisements contained colorful photographs of stars in their costumes. The stars accepted the assignments without pay. To them, the publicity was more important.

Almost overnight, women began to smoke in public. The taboo had been broken. Several months later, several companies that manufactured candies placed advertisements informing customers that smoking was not good for their health. Lasker reacted by seeing Hill, and, together, they came up with the line "Reach for a Lucky instead of a Sweet," which was added to the "precious voice" advertisements. Within a few years, Lucky Strike was the best-selling cigarette, and Lord and Thomas earned millions from the account.

In 1926 Lord and Thomas became Lord and Thomas and Logan when Lasker asked Thomas F. Logan, who owned the Logan agency, to consolidate with Lord and Thomas. Through Logan, Lord and Thomas acquired some excellent accounts, including the Radio Corporation of America (RCA), which was headed by David Sarnoff, whom Lasker had met. Sarnoff had been instrumental in creating the National Broadcasting Company (NBC) in 1926. As radio became popular, programs were created and eventually sponsored by advertisers. Lasker had an hour-long program created for one of his accounts, Palmolive. When this proved successful, he had programs created for other sponsors. By 1928, the year Logan died, Lord and Thomas was responsible for about 50 percent of the advertising placed with NBC. Other programs were created for other advertisers, including *Amos 'n' Andy* for Pepsodent, *The Story of Mary Marlin* for Kleenex, and *Information Please* for Lucky Strike. With the help of radio, Lasker's Lord and Thomas agency became the largest advertising agency in the world in the 1930s.

While the country faced the depression, Lasker's Lord and Thomas advertising agency continued, but at a slower pace. In 1931 Lasker cut salaries by 25 percent. Two years later he fired more than 50 employees. Was the depression taking its toll on Lasker? Was it age? Or was it worry?

In 1936 Flora died, and Albert Lasker was distraught. The love of his life had left him alone. Lasker was 56. What would he do? Advertising was no longer interesting to him. By 1938 he retired from Lord and Thomas, and Don Francisco succeeded him as president. Lasker resumed the position when Francisco left the agency to go to work for the government. Pearl Harbor had been bombed by the Japanese, and the country faced another world war.

During his brief retirement, however, Lasker met an actress,

Doris Kenyon, in California and, after a few weeks, married her. The marriage ended in divorce within a year. In 1939 he met Mary Woodard Reinhardt in New York. They dated for more than a year, then married. Lasker realized that Mary had interests similar to his; she could talk to him about politics, business, and religion. He realized, too, that Mary's love saved him from losing his mind.

Two years later he informed her that he was going to retire from the agency. According to John Gunther, there were several reasons for his desiring to retire:

First, he was . . . tired. Second, he was bored. Third, the new generation of executives with whom he had to deal seemed far beneath his standards. Fourth, he wanted to devote himself to public service. Fifth, he felt that shortages induced by the war effort were bound to curtail sales of consumer goods, on which his business largely depended. Sixth . . . , Edward [his son] had made it clear that he did not wish to succeed his father in the business, and would not return to advertising after the war.[16]

Lasker met with his three senior executives, Emerson Foote, Fairfax Cone, and Don Belding, and the agency Lord and Thomas soon became Foote, Cone, and Belding. Lasker informed the agency's major clients of his decision and persuaded most to stay with the new company.

Lord and Thomas as an advertising agency died on December 30, 1942. Albert Lasker, who believed that a good advertisement must have a central idea, news, and enough creativity to make the central idea sing, died from cancer 10 years later. He was 72 years of age.

Under Lasker's guidance, Lord and Thomas handled such clients as the Wilson Ear Drum Company, the "1900" Washer Company, the Quaker Oats Company, the Pepsodent Company, the Sunkist Growers, Inc., the B. P. Johnson Soap Company, the Van Camp Packing Company, Goodyear, Kimberly-Clark, the Radio Corporation of America, and the American Tobacco Company.

NOTES

1. Stephen Fox, *The Mirror Makers: A History of American Advertising and Its Creators* (New York: William Morrow and Co. 1984), p. 40.

2. Albert D. Lasker, "Reminiscences," Columbia Oral History Collection, 1949–1950, p. 7.

3. Albert D. Lasker, "The Personal Reminiscences of Albert Lasker," *American Heritage* (December 1954), p. 78.

4. *The Saturday Evening Post*, Vol. 173, No. 28 (January 12, 1901), p. 18.

5. Albert D. Lasker, *The Lasker Story . . . As He Told It* (Chicago: Advertising Publications, 1963), p. 19.

6. Fox, *The Mirror Makers*, p. 50.

7. John Gunther, *Taken at the Flood: The Story of Albert D. Lasker* (New York: Harper and Brothers, 1960), p. 60.

8. Fox, *The Mirror Makers*, p. 51.

9. Lasker, "Reminiscences," p. 79.

10. Lasker, *The Lasker Story*, p. 38.

11. Don Belding, "End of an Era in Advertising," *Advertising Agency and Advertising and Selling* (July 1952), p. 67.

12. Advertisement 37, April 21, 1927. From Foote, Cone and Belding's file of Lord and Thomas original advertisements.

13. Gunther, *Taken at the Flood*, p. 155.

14. Lasker, "The Personal Reminiscences of Albert Lasker," p. 82.

15. Ibid., p. 84.

16. Gunther, *Taken at the Flood*, p. 269.

7

Procter & Gamble and Advertising Cleanliness: The First 100 Years

INTRODUCTION

Cleanliness in the United States became somewhat of a concern in the late 1700s, and baths, which allowed total immersion, were installed in various cities. Prior to this time men bathed in creeks, rivers, lakes, and oceans. Women, for the most part, primarily because it was a social taboo, were denied this privilege. They bathed sporadically in private, usually with a piece of cloth and water. However, when bathhouses opened, most admitted women. These bathhouses emphasized cleanliness, not cold or mineral or spring water, which had been emphasized by so-called mineral spring spas that had been established by the 1770s.[1]

Man's interest in cleanliness dates to antiquity, but tradition was not necessarily the reason for cleanliness to become a major concern in the late 1700s. Although various religions had survived hundreds, if not thousands, of years and had perpetuated, to a certain extent, cleanliness of the body as well as the mind or spirit, most people had been hindered from practicing what their ministers had occasionally preached. Only the wealthy, for instance, could afford in-house bathrooms, and this was in the late 1700s, when tubs and elements of modern plumbing became available in certain cities of the country. However, the primary reason for cleanliness to grow in importance was the genteel code of behavior, which people adopted and/or taught to others.

Manuals concerning gentility were published for the betterment of mankind. Some of these manuals actually appeared in the American colonies during the early 1700s; apparently, certain Americans desired to change their values and, subsequently, their culture. Certain American groups such as the American gentry patterned themselves after their European counterparts. What revolutionary innovations appeared in England, for instance, were eventually brought to America. Even certain sanitary habits made their way across the Atlantic. According to Bushman and Bushman:

This wave of fashion reached the American shore in the 1790s intermingled with all the currents of influences that flowed so freely from England to America. Tubs in a variety of designs were on the market in London, and American tinsmiths made them available in Philadelphia at the same time. Regular, year-around bathing was certainly not routine even in the most elite households in either England or America by 1800.[2]

Cleanliness grew in popularity throughout the 1800s, and cold baths were claimed to benefit those with certain medical ailments such as consequent indigestion, while warm or hot baths were claimed to benefit those with certain medical problems such as anxiety. As the medical community learned more about the human anatomy, certain physicians encouraged their patients and others to take warm or hot baths so dirt and germs would be removed from the skin. However, most Americans did not take baths on a regular basis until around 1850 or later. Even though cleanliness "ranked as a mark of moral superiority and dirtiness as a sign of degradation,"[3] most Americans refused to take the time or did not believe that bathing was *that* important or even beneficial. Many Americans did not believe that bathing was necessary in order to function as a productive member of society. Nonetheless, if a person aspired to be accepted into the middle or upper class, he or she had to be clean; this was an absolute requirement.

As the 1800s passed, the demand for soap grew. As a result, certain companies introduced to the American public bars of soap for cleansing the body. One of these companies, Procter & Gamble, was founded in Cincinnati, Ohio.

THE MANUFACTURING OF SOAP IN AMERICA

The making of soap in America was done by the housewife for many years. She used the fats she collected and made soft soap that was used by every member of her family. Eventually, craftsmen who knew how to make soap from fats and ashes arrived in the colonies. For many years, however, these craftsmen exported the soap ashes and made candles for the colonists.

According to Samuel Colgate, even though small soap-boiling establishments had been founded in large towns by 1795, most of these establishments earned very little from making and selling soap because most soap was made at home.[4]

As the 1800s progressed, more Americans purchased soap from these small firms. In addition, these firms exported soap as well as candles. In 1835, for instance, exports of these products totaled $534,467.[5] Seven years later these firms were producing "50,000,000 pounds of soap, 18,000,000 pounds of tallow candles, and 3,000,000 pounds of wax and spermaceti candles."[6] Exports of these products totaled more than $1 million.[7]

The early soaps were made from various fats such as stearine, palmitine, and oleine. Alkalis were mixed with the fats for the purpose of varying the hardness. Soda, for instance, made a harder soap than potash. Stearine mixed with soda made the hardest soap, while oleine and potash made the softest soap. Oils, too, were used in manufacturing soap. These included olive oil, palm oil, and linseed oil. Other ingredients were added, depending on the purpose of the soap.

THE FOUNDING OF PROCTER & GAMBLE

Procter & Gamble, one of the best-known companies in the world, was founded by William Procter and James Gamble in Cincinnati, Ohio, in 1837. Procter, a lean man with a black beard, knew how to make candles. Gamble, a short man with a clean-shaven face, knew how to make soap. Although Procter's name is presented first in the company's name, he was not the first of the two to arrive in the United States.

James Gamble was born in Ireland. His father, George Gamble, was a Methodist minister who desired to escape with his family the depression that gripped Ireland in 1819. George had heard about abundant prosperity in, of all places, Shawneetown, Illinois. Friends and others who had journeyed to America and to this small town had written to him about their good fortune. George, determined to leave his unfortunate predicament behind, loaded his family onto a ship and sailed across the Atlantic to America.

George and his family journeyed safely to Pittsburgh; however, their funds were in short supply. The only form of transportation that would take them west and that they could afford was a flatboat on the Ohio River, which they boarded after some hesitation. James, 16, got violently ill as the flatboat moved almost silently downstream. Finally, after several days, the boat stopped in Cincinnati, Ohio, and the family went ashore. James, still ill, needed to rest. Members of the family were undoubtedly amazed at the bustling city that bordered the river. Although shipbuilding dominated the edge of the river, the city had various brewing companies as well as other businesses. The slaughter of swine was a major industry. Cincinnati was a very busy city in the early 1800s, even though Horace Greeley et al. pointed out that

Cincinnati ... had in 1800 only four hundred inhabitants, the disputed title to the territory which then formed what was called the Northwest Territory having proved an obstacle in the way of its rapid settlement. With the settlement of this question, the West was opened freely to the tide of emigration which flowed from the Eastern States, caused by the attractions of the new life of a new country, and the opportunities it afforded for enterprise, together with that from Europe, composed of those who looked with hope to the new republic, and sought to live where the simple right of political representation which it required a revolution to obtain at home was freely offered to any one who desired it.[8]

The family remained in Cincinnati. At first, they used the excuse that James was ill. Then they used the excuse that Cincinnati offered employment. George, for instance, opened a greenhouse and occasionally preached. James worked briefly for his father, then became an apprentice to William Bell, a soap manufacturer. James Gamble worked for Bell for eight years until he and Hiram Knowlton, a friend, opened a soap and candle shop. The business, though small, was profitable, and James, who had met Elizabeth Ann Norris, the daughter of a successful candlemaker, Alexander Norris, eventually married her. He was 30.

Norris had another daughter, Olivia, who married William Procter the same year. Procter had owned a woolen goods store in England until burglars stole every item in the shop; Procter owed creditors approximately $8,000.

Procter promised to pay his creditors as soon as he could and sailed with his wife, Martha, to America. Like George Gamble, he, too, had heard about unlimited opportunity in the New World, except the place he had heard about was called "the falls of Ohio," which was actually Louisville, Kentucky. Procter and his wife, like the Gambles, boarded a flatboat on the Ohio River; their destination was "the falls of Ohio." Unfortunately, before they could make it to Louisville, Martha contracted cholera. When the boat stopped in Cincinnati, Procter took his wife to one doctor, then another. The prognosis was the same: there was nothing that could be done for her. Martha died within several days. Stricken with grief and possibly feeling responsible for his wife's death, Procter buried Martha. However, he did not go to "the falls of Ohio." He remained in Cincinnati and accepted a position at a bank. Procter soon realized that his wages were insufficient; he could not live on what he earned and pay his creditors. He also realized that Cincinnati provided a very good opportunity to those who knew how to make candles.

Procter relied on the skills he had learned as a child. He made candles and sold them in a small store, which he rented. Procter, probably because he was alone, was consumed by his business. When he met Olivia Norris, he was earning a good living and paying his creditors. Procter realized that Olivia could fill the void that had been caused by Martha's death, so he asked her to marry him; Olivia graciously and formally accepted.

William Procter and James Gamble were brothers-in-law, and they were purchasing the same animal fats. In essence, they were competing for the same raw material to produce their respective products. This fact seemed illogical to their father-in-law. He persuaded them to become partners, even though he knew that Gamble had a partner.

In 1837 Gamble's partnership with Knowlton ended, and Gamble moved his share of the goods into Procter's store. Although Gamble and Procter had not signed a formal contract, they worked as partners nonetheless. The same year they purchased the land for their candle and soap factory.

The firm, though small, prospered. Advertising was placed infrequently in local newspapers. The first advertisement, for instance, appeared in the *Cincinnati Gazette* on June 29, 1838; it was two inches in length:

Oils for lamps and machinery. A fine article of clarified Pig's Foot Oil, equal to sperm, at a low price and in quantities to suit buyers. Neat's Foot oil ditto. Also No. 1 & 2 soap. Palm and shaving ditto. For sale by Procter & Gamble Co., east side Main Street 2nd door off 6th Street.[9]

Gamble was responsible for production, and Procter was responsible for sales. Production was crude and primitive. Sales increased over the months, and the collection of fats and potash had to be extended to other areas outside Cincinnati.

Procter and Gamble, primarily because of competition, realized that if they purchased greater quantities of raw materials, they would not find themselves in the precarious position of not having any products to sell. They also realized that if they remained ethical in their advertising, they would invariably prosper. The principles of their Protestant religion were applied to their advertising and to their business overall.

The firm continued to prosper. By 1848, for instance, Procter & Gamble, though still small, was earning $26,000 annually.

STARS AND THE MAN IN THE MOON

In the 1980s and 1990s a rumor suggesting that the president of Procter & Gamble had sold his soul to Satan was spread by certain individuals, including several who sold products manufactured by Amway. According to the rumor, the president of the company had proved his allegiance to Satan by having the figure "666" placed on the company's trademark, which appeared on every product's package. In return for his devotion and soul, Satan allowed the company to prosper. As a result of the company's prosperity, the church of Satan was awarded a percentage of the company's profits.

The company, which received thousands of telephone calls from consumers inquiring about the rumor's validity, launched a public relations campaign to quash the rumor in the 1980s. Then the company successfully sued several individuals for passing out literature that stated Procter & Gamble supported the church of Satan. Nonetheless, the rumor continued to rear its ugly head. Each time the rumor surfaced, hundreds, if not thousands, of telephone calls from concerned consumers bothered the company. Procter & Gamble, which had modified its trademark over the years, modified the design once again in 1991. The company restricted the design's usage to buildings, certain awards, and the company's stationery. What had appeared on every product's package for almost a century was retired.[10]

The symbol that became the company's trademark actually germinated from the crude black crosses that illiterate wharf hands had painted on boxes of Procter & Gamble Star candles in 1851. The wharf hands painted the boxes for identification purposes. Eventually, wharf hands changed the crosses to stars, then painted circles around the stars. Later, part of a man's face was painted inside the circles.

Procter and Gamble approved of the "moon and stars" symbol and had it painted on each box; however, later, they decided to have the "man in the moon" removed, until a merchant in New Orleans rejected a particular shipment because he believed the shipment of boxes to contain imitations. William Procter learned of the merchant's legitimate concern and had the "man in the moon" added to the symbol. In addition, he requested that the cluster of stars number 13, for the original 13 colonies, which had been represented by 13 stars in the first flag of the United States.

In 1875 the company's executives realized the importance of the symbol and several years later, as soon as it was possible, registered the trademark with the newly opened Patent Office. The design was sculpted at least twice, in 1882 and again in 1930. The design sculpted in 1930 was used on the company's products' packages until it was retired as a result of the persistent rumor.

THE GROWTH OF PROCTER & GAMBLE

Horace Greeley et al. wrote:

Fifty years after the opening of this century, less than the time allotted for two generations, the population of Cincinnati had increased from four hundred to nearly two hundred thousand persons, had built nearly a thousand steamboats, and shipped yearly nearly one hundred millions of dollars' worth of produce, importing nearly eighty millions of dollars' worth of materials from abroad. Beside this, the industrial enterprise of the city had built up a manufacturing interest which produced an aggregate of over fifty millions of dollars' worth of various articles, and the city has established railroad connection with more than ten thousand miles of railroad leading directly to or through it.[11]

Procter & Gamble's sales increased, and the two industrious partners realized that a larger facility was required. In addition to concentrating on their Star candles, which were made from pork fats, the partners developed two new soaps from the "red oil" or oleic acid that was actually a by-product of the Star candle process. For instance, they used the red oil to produce a hard, white soap that was referred to as Mottled German. Later, they used the red oil to produce a hard, rough soap called Oleine.

William Procter's oldest son, William Alexander Procter, left college in 1851 and went to work for James Gamble, his uncle, in the factory. William worked so diligently that the partners offered him 10 percent of the business six years later.

Although Procter and Gamble attempted several times to extract glycerin from the wastewater, they were not successful until 1858, when Richard Tilghman, a chemist, showed them how. Procter and Gamble licensed the process from Tilghman and eventually sold glycerin at a much lower price than their competitors.

George H. Procter, who had attended Kenyon College, joined the company as a sales representative and successfully increased the sales of Mottled German and Oleine soaps. To better illustrate Procter & Gamble's progress, Charles Cist, in his *Sketches and Statistics of Cincinnati in 1859*, wrote:

Procter & Gamble . . . are probably engaged more extensively in manufacturing operations, than any other establishment in our city. They consume seven hundred barrels rosin, and three hundred tons soda ash; ten thousand carboys—or six hundred thousand pounds—sulphuric acid; one hundred and fifteen thousand pounds candle-wick, and thirty thousand barrels, of two hundred and fifty pounds each—or seven million five hundred thousand pounds—lard, annually, in their various products.

Their sales have largely exceeded one million dollars yearly; and in consequence of the high price of the great staple, lard, will this year, doubtless, reach much higher figures than heretofore. They employ eighty hands, in the various departments of their business.[12]

In 1860, realizing that a war was imminent, Procter and Gamble sent William and James Norris Gamble, his cousin, to New Orleans to purchase a large supply of rosin, which was necessary for making soap. Procter and Gamble desired to have enough supplies on hand in case trade routes were cut off by troops.

When the Civil War erupted several months later, Procter & Gamble had more supplies than their competitors for making soap. The Union Army contracted with the company, and Procter & Gamble had to supply 1,000 cases of soap a day. The company hired additional people and purchased more equipment and buildings in order to meet the terms of the contract.

Procter & Gamble faced numerous obstacles, however, including a fire that destroyed part of the factory and a shortage of rosin. Even though the factory closed every Sunday, the company met its commitment.

When the war ended, Procter and Gamble assumed that orders for their products would decrease substantially. That was not the case. Men, particularly those who had served in the Union Army, had used Procter & Gamble products for four years; therefore, many purchased the products after the war. In addition, certain merchants in the South had purchased the products before the war; even if they could not afford to pay cash, these merchants were extended credit by the company.

Procter & Gamble continued to grow and prosper; the company added new markets and developed new products. However, the original founders of the company were in their mid-60s. By 1867, when the company was 30 years old, both men relied on their sons to manage the business.

Two years later, when a few speculators attempted to capture the gold market, President Ulysses S. Grant sold $4 million of the government's gold in an effort to drive down the price. As a result of the decrease, investors on Wall Street panicked, which caused the entire country to suffer. People saved what little money they had; many refused to purchase certain goods as well as pay their debts. Like other companies at the time, Procter & Gamble's sales decreased. Profits, too, plummeted, and the company suffered. It actually operated in the red for a year, even though it reduced the number of employees.

The same year Harley Thomas Procter, another son of William Procter, began to work as a sales representative at the company. Harley, 21, desired to see Procter & Gamble rebound. The company's sales did not increase until the early 1870s.

In the late 1870s, the company developed Ivory soap, which was heavily advertised by Harley Procter. As a result of his promotional efforts, the soap became the company's best-selling product. (The development and advertising of Ivory soap are discussed later in this chapter.)

Procter & Gamble's factory burned in January 1884. Partner James Gamble and members of the two families broke ground on a new, much larger factory, appropriately named Ivorydale, in 1885. The new factory's production capacity for soap was more than twice the production capacity of the former factory, which had been 200,000 bars a day. In addition to Ivory and several other brands, the company produced Lenox, a new laundry soap that had been developed by James Norris Gamble. Harley Procter was responsible for the product's advertising, which included in-store promotions. As a result of Harley's efforts, sales of Lenox increased; it became the company's second best-selling soap.

In 1887 the only son of William Alexander Procter, William

Cooper Procter, who had attended the College of New Jersey (now Princeton University) and who had worked in the factory, informed his father that factory employees worked too many hours and suggested that the workers have Saturday afternoons off. Cooper, as he was called, argued that the workers would actually work harder as a result. Although Cooper's father and uncle disagreed, Harley Procter, who liked the idea, was able to persuade Cooper's father and James Norris that the company should at least test the proposal. The proposal was tested, but a minority of workers desired more. At this period, laborers across the country were uniting and making revolutionary demands of their employers. Procter & Gamble's employees went on strike numerous times during the next several years. Cooper suggested that the company should allow its employees a share of the profits, a radical idea that was immediately rejected. However, certain writers who wrote for business magazines learned about the idea and requested interviews. Cooper firmly believed that his plan, if implemented, would result in greater productivity on the part of the employees.

The plan was accepted and explained to the employees later that year. A minority of workers thought the plan was merely a ploy to get them to stop complaining and to work harder. Most employees, especially when the dividends were handed out several months later, appreciated the extra income. The plan did not necessarily cause employees to work harder or more efficiently, as Cooper had predicted. On the other hand, the number of strikes decreased. Ida Tarbell discussed the plan in detail:

An equally notable venture in profit sharing was that undertaken by Procter and Gamble, the soap manufacturers in Cincinnati. As they frankly informed their employees, the purpose was to increase "diligence, carefulness and thoughtful cooperation" in order to enlarge earnings—earnings in which, of course, the employees would share. The sum divided was to bear the same relation to the total profits as the amount of wages, including the partners' salaries, bore to the total cost of carrying on the business. Only those who had been three months or more with the firm were to participate. The semiannual day of distribution was set aside as a holiday.

In May, 1890, on the sixth dividend day, it was reported that profits of sixty thousand dollars had been distributed in the three preceding years, equal to about sixteen per cent of the wages paid. The "diligence, carefulness and thoughtful cooperation" which the firm sought had not, however, been fully secured. Certain changes were therefore made in the plan: the employees were divided into four classes, and dividends were to follow merit. But the revised regulations did not work out as well as the company desired. Just before and after dividend days enthusiasm was great; the diligence was all that could be asked. But gradually this wore off, to return only as the next celebration approached.[13]

The same year Harley James Morrison, a graduate of Yale, was hired to help develop new products. Within three years he persuaded Procter & Gamble executives to build a laboratory at Ivorydale. This laboratory was responsible for scientific inquiry that was conducted for the purpose of developing new products and improving old products.

The company, which was divided equally among the Procters and Gambles, continued to prosper under the second generation's guidance.

Later, in 1887, Cooper Procter was given a small interest in the company. Perhaps it was because of his receiving an interest in the company or that his previous idea was ultimately accepted and implemented that he suggested the partnership become a public corporation.

The first stockholders' meeting was held three years later, in 1890, and 11 members were elected to the board of directors. Five of these members included William Alexander Procter, James Norris Gamble, Harley T. Procter, David B. Gamble, and William Cooper Procter. Founder James Gamble was 87 and too old to serve. Other members of the board were not related to the Procters or the Gambles and were not elected officials of the company. As a result, the management of the company remained in the families' control.

Founder James Gamble died in 1891, and Harley T. Procter, 43, informed William Alexander Procter and other members of the families that he was retiring. They attempted to persuade him to remain, but he was determined to move to New England with his wife and breed horses, which he did. The advertising campaigns for which he had been responsible continued. Full-page advertisements with illustrations of Ivory appeared in the major publications of the day, and the company continued to prosper.

Although William Alexander Procter was president, his son William Cooper Procter was general manager and consequently searched for professionals who knew how to manage certain departments and employees. He initiated a stock-purchasing plan for employees that was guaranteed by the company and later coupled with the profit-sharing plan.

Procter & Gamble continued to expand as a result of developing new products and sales. In 1903, for instance, the company built another plant in Kansas City. In 1906 the company built Port Ivory in New York. Ivory and Lenox soaps were the company's best-selling brands, but other companies were advertising successfully other brands of soap such as Pears'. Procter & Gamble responded to these companies by developing products such as P & G White Naphtha and by increasing its advertising budget.

William Alexander Procter, who had been grieving for several years for his deceased wife, killed himself in 1907. His son, William Cooper Procter, became president at a time when numerous companies closed or decreased the number of employees as a result of several large banks' closing in New York. Procter & Gamble weathered the storm that gripped the nation. Cooper, who actually learned about hydrogenation from E. C. Kayser, a German chemical engineer who had turned liquid cottonseed oil into a solid, purchased the rights to use Kayser's hydrogenation process and subsequently had a facility built at Ivorydale in 1908. The product that was developed in the new facility was Crisco, a new vegetable shortening, which ultimately could be found in most American kitchens.

During World War I, Procter & Gamble, in an effort to compete successfully against Lever Brothers, expanded into Canada when it had a factory built in 1914 in Hamilton, Ontario. The facility produced Ivory soap and Crisco.

In 1917 the plant in Kansas City closed when picketers dared any employee to cross the picket line. Cooper Procter boarded a train for Kansas City, met with a committee of employees, and listened attentively to their demands. As a result of the meeting, Cooper agreed to an eight-hour workday, which would be enacted as soon as the war ended. The committee agreed to his terms, and the plant immediately reopened.

Cooper Procter enacted the Employees' Conference Plan, which encouraged a representative body of employees to meet frequently with upper management to discuss issues and resolve problems, in 1918. The Employees' Conference Plan worked until 1937, when the U.S. Supreme Court ruled that the National Labor Relations Act of 1935 was constitutional. Conference committees had to be abolished. Procter & Gamble complied.

The same year the company began selling its products directly to retailers. The plan was fought by various companies, especially wholesalers. Nonetheless, Procter & Gamble increased its sales staff and opened various warehouses across the country. Unfortunately, a recession hit the country in the early 1920s, and Procter & Gamble lost at least $30 million.

In 1923, however, the company rebounded. Its direct selling plan, for instance, had been improved and had been accepted by more companies. Its manufacturing output had increased. Employees realized they had a certain security.

In addition, the company introduced new products such as Ivory Flakes for washing dishes and laundering certain fabrics, Chipso for various kinds of cleaning, including laundering, and Camay soap for the bathroom. This brand of soap competed with Ivory and was heavily advertised. Even samples were delivered door-to-door, and housewives were asked to write to the company to inform executives about the product.

The same year the company established an economic research department primarily for the purpose of studying the commodities markets. The department, under Dr. D. Paul Smelser, conducted surveys of various kinds and learned what consumers believed about new and old products manufactured by Procter & Gamble. Other forms of market research were used to learn about advertising, particularly its effectiveness. Regional market tests were conducted before any new product was sold nationally. Several products failed these tests and were discontinued.

Although William Cooper Procter was president of the company, he realized that he was growing older. Richard R. Deupree, who had been hired in 1905 as an office boy and who had served as a salesman, manager of the Bulk Soap Sales Division, manager of western sales for all consumer products, general sales manager, and a director, was made general manager in 1927, then a vice president a year later. Procter allowed Deupree to assume responsibility of managing the company. In 1930 William Cooper Procter was named chairman, and Deupree was elected president. Procter was 68, and Deupree was 45. In 1933 Deupree, at Cooper's urging, enacted a five-day, 40-hour workweek at every Procter & Gamble factory. A year later William Cooper Procter, 71, died.

The Great Depression gripped the country. Although Procter & Gamble's sales plummeted, Deupree refused to slash the company's advertising budget. Indeed, Deupree and the company's advertising manager, Ralph Rogan, through the Blackman Company, an advertising agency in New York, had advertised Crisco on several radio programs as early as 1923. Eventually, as radio grew in popularity, Procter & Gamble advertised other products such as Ivory on several early serials, which were actually developed for the company's products. The company was also responsible for developing the "slice-of-life" advertising format that was adopted later by other companies.

By the time the company was 100 years old in 1937, Procter & Gamble's products were known to millions, and sales of certain products had more than doubled when the Great Depression ended. Between 1933 and 1935, for instance, net earnings increased 66 percent.

In 1937, when the company celebrated its centennial birthday, the Ohio River flooded parts of Cincinnati, including parts of Ivorydale. Even though Mother Nature was unkind to some of Procter & Gamble's facilities, the company was experiencing phenomenal growth, with 11 factories in the United States and 5 in four other countries. Procter & Gamble's growth was primarily the result of research in its manufacturing, advertising, and sales departments and in the quality of its personnel.[14]

THE ADVERTISING OF IVORY SOAP FROM THE 1880s TO THE 1930s

During the 1870s James Norris Gamble and Procter & Gamble's first full-time chemist from England, a man by the name of

Gibson, were attempting to make a hard, white soap that would be as good as the castile soaps of Europe. The company purchased a formula from another soap manufacturer, then experimented with it. Major changes were made to the formula. Finally, in 1878, James Gamble announced that his laboratory had achieved what had seemed to some in the company impossible. He and his associates had created a formula that met everyone's expectations. Although the new soap was to be marketed as P & G White Soap, Harley Procter instinctively realized that the name was not unique or memorable. He informed other members of the family that the product needed a name that people would remember. They gave the task of naming the product to him. Harley eagerly read Dr. Roget's thesaurus and the dictionary. Nothing. He read countless lists of names for other products, including soaps. Nothing. Finally, at church one Sunday morning the minister read Psalms 45:8: "All thy garments smell of myrrh and aloes and cassia, out of the ivory palaces whereby they have made thee glad." The word "ivory" remained in Harley's mind, probably because it was white, and Harley realized that white symbolized cleanliness, if not purity. He also realized that "ivory" was expensive. Harley decided that "Ivory" would be the best name for Procter & Gamble's white soap. According to the editors of *Advertising Age*, "Harley Procter . . . asked a New York chemist to analyze the three leading brands of castile soap, then asked that same chemist to evaluate Ivory. By the chemist's own definition of purity, Ivory was purer than the castiles, with only 0.56% impurities."[15]

Before the soap was successfully marketed, one of the men who handled one of the crutchers forgot to stop the machine when he went to lunch. Crutchers contained arms that mixed the ingredients for the soap. Upon his return, the mixture was frothy and overflowing the vat. However, his superior decided that the ingredients had not been changed and subsequently used the mixture for soap, which was eventually shipped. One or two months later merchants were requesting the "soap that floats." Unfortunately, no one at the company knew which brand of soap these merchants were requesting until a thorough investigation revealed the "accidental" mixture, which was repeated. The company then produced the "soap that floats."

Although Harley Procter, who was now sales manager for the company, was informed that Ivory would float, he was not necessarily impressed. He focused on the soap's color as well as its gentleness. Of course, he included the fact that it was 99.44 percent pure. In addition, he requested funds for advertising directly to consumers, which was a relatively new concept to American manufacturers. Procter & Gamble had been spending about $1,500 a year on advertising to merchants. The company's executives agreed to listen to his rationale but were not convinced that his explanation was sound. Harley reiterated his idea, and in 1882 the partners increased the advertising budget to $11,000. Immediately, Harley, who had been responsible for the notch in the middle of the large-size bar so that the consumers could break it into two smaller bars and who had been responsible for the checkerboard wrapper with the word "Ivory" and the company's trademark, created the first consumer advertisement for Ivory soap. The advertisement appeared in the December 21, 1882 issue of the religious publication *The Independent*:

THE "IVORY" is a Laundry Soap, with all the fine qualities of a choice Toilet Soap, and is 99 44–100 per cent. **pure**.

Ladies will find this Soap especially adapted for washing laces, infants' clothing, silk hose, cleaning gloves and all articles of fine texture and delicate color, and for the varied uses about the house that daily arise, requiring the use of soap that is above the ordinary in quality.

For the Bath, Toilet, or Nursery it is preferred to most of the Soaps sold for toilet use, being purer and much more pleasant and effective and possessing all the desirable properties of the finest unadulterated White Castile Soap. The Ivory Soap will "**float**."

The cakes are so shaped that they may be used entire for general purposes or divided with a stout thread (as illustrated) into two perfectly formed cakes, of convenient size for toilet use.

The price, compared to the quality and the size of the cakes, makes it the cheapest Soap for everybody for every want. TRY IT.
SOLD EVERYWHERE[16]

The illustration, which was above the copy, contained a pair of hands tying a string around a large bar of soap. The string was in the notched area.

Harley Procter placed advertisements in the more popular

women's service magazines such as *Good Housekeeping* and the *Ladies' Home Journal*. He urged readers to purchase a bar of Ivory for each room in the house. He did not use the fact that Ivory soap would float and the "99 44–100 percent pure" claim in every advertisement, however. The fact that the soap would float was not emphasized in advertisements until about 10 years later. Nonetheless, Harley's early advertisements were so successful that certain Procter & Gamble competitors mentioned Ivory by name in comparative advertisements for their respective products.

In the March 1886, issue of the *Ladies' Home Journal*, a quarter-page advertisement announced the Ivory soap etching, which was available for 54¢ to cover packaging and postage, from Procter & Gamble. One of the first premiums that was offered to consumers was the Ivory soap "Watch Charm," which was a small facsimile of a bar of Ivory soap with a gold-plated ring, for the centerpiece from 12 soap wrappers. This advertisement appeared in the January 1889 issue of the *Ladies' Home Journal*.

In addition to these advertisements, Harley persuaded the company to sponsor a contest for amateur poets. The writer of the best poem would receive $300. The contest generated thousands of submissions, and sales of Ivory increased substantially. Harley's ideas for selling Ivory seemed endless, at least to others in the company.

In the January 6, 1894, issue of *Harper's Weekly*, the company placed a one-third column advertisement that contained the words "Ivory soap" with an illustration of the notched bar. Two lines of copy—"It Floats" and "For Table Linen"—immediately followed. Other advertisements during this period were similar in the sense that each mentioned an article found in the kitchen or dining room that could be cleaned with Ivory soap.

In the January 5, 1895, issue of *Harper's Weekly*, the following advertisement appeared:

Ivory
Soap
99 44/100 Pure

Why not wash with pure white Ivory Soap and have pure white linen? "Whatever is worth doing at all, is worth doing well."[17]

This advertisement emphasized the color and the article on which the product could be applied.

In 1896 the advertisements for Ivory discussed uses other than cleaning, as the following illustrates:

TO BICYCLISTS:

Many of those who have made the discovery have requested us to notify wheelmen generally that there is no better chain lubricant than Ivory Soap; it is the most cleanly application and is perfect for this use.

An additional block of copy in smaller size type discussed the product's ingredients:

The vegetable oils of which Ivory Soap is made, and its purity, fit it for many special uses for which other soaps are unsafe and unsatisfactory. Ivory Soap is sold by more dealers and used in more households than any other.[18]

The last sentence informed the consumer that unless she had Ivory in her home, she was not purchasing the preferred brand.

In the December 1897 issue of the *Ladies' Home Journal*, a quarter-page advertisement contained a large illustration of Mrs. S. T. Roper, an authority on the selection and preparation of food, who endorsed Ivory:

With the increase of wealth and luxury there comes an increased demand for a better and safer cleansing agent for household use. A large number of housekeepers have discarded the ordinary colored soaps and are now using only a pure soap of the best quality. Mrs. S. T. Roper, widely known as an authority on the selection and preparation of food and other articles of household consumption, says [the quotation was in smaller size type]: "In looking over the field I am sure that the housewife can afford without a second thought to throw away her alkali powders, drop her ammonia bottle, and use Ivory Soap for all purposes, with far better results than could be obtained from combinations of which she knows but little."[19]

Advertisements featuring other authorities discussing Ivory appeared in magazines at this time and were similarly designed.

Harley Procter pioneered the use of preprinted color inserts in the early magazines when he hired the Procter and Collier Company, which was actually a printing firm in Cincinnati, in 1900. The firm was hired to produce four-color advertisements. These advertisements contained colorful illustrations that had been drawn by the most popular artists of the day, such as Alice Barber Stephens and Maxfield Parrish. Reproductions of these commissioned works of art were available for Ivory wrappers.

Harley Procter also asked consumers how they used Ivory in their homes. Procter & Gamble received numerous suggestions, and Harley Procter used many of these in advertisements. Later, the company published and advertised the booklet *Unusual Uses of Ivory Soap*, which contained many of the suggestions that had been mailed to the company. Other booklets followed, including *Questions Often Asked*, which was published in 1900.

Advertisements featuring babies in illustrations became well known and attracted attention. The Ivory babies, as they were called, implied that the soap was so mild that mothers could use it to wash their infants.

Before 1910, advertisements for Ivory were encouraging consumers to use the product five or six times a day to improve their complexion.

In the July 1910 issue of the *Ladies' Home Journal*, the following advertisement occupied a full page:

No matter whether you bathe in the morning or at night, in warm water or cold, *you should use Ivory Soap.*
It floats. It is pure. It lathers freely. It rinses easily. It *cleans!*
Can you think of any other qualities that a bath soap should have?
Ivory Soap . . . . It Floats.[20]

The copy emphasized the name of the product and the fact that the product cleans. The phrase "Ivory Soap . . . It Floats" was printed in large, bold letters. A large illustration of a woman preparing to take a bath was above the block of copy. She was holding a bar of Ivory in her left hand and looking at the reader.

In 1915 the company's advertisements for Ivory claimed that the product was gentle enough for babies, as the following advertisement illustrates:

Babies and Ivory Soap seem to belong to each other. It is natural to think of Ivory Soap in connection with a baby's tender skin and it is almost impossible not to think of baby's bath when recalling the many particular things which Ivory does so well. [The remaining blocks of copy were in smaller size type.] The sensitive little body demands a soap that is mild and pure, above all else. To most people Ivory has come to mean the mildest and purest soap that can be made. Users of Ivory Soap now think of it as the soap for all better-than-ordinary purposes. They know that it is capable of the most exacting things—that even the tender skin of a new baby is unhurt by its use.

The Ivory Soap "Baby Book" is a valuable treatise on the raising of healthy, happy children. You may have a copy free of charge by addressing The Procter & Gamble Company, Dept. 3-B, Cincinnati, Ohio.

Ivory Soap. . . . It Floats. . . . 99 44/100% Pure[21]

The block of copy appeared on an illustration of an unopened scroll. A large illustration of a woman and her babies was in a frame that rested above the scroll. The advertisement's design was undoubtedly influenced by artists who had drawn or painted religious artifacts or figures centuries before.

In the 1920s, the advertising focused on hair, certain articles of clothing, and skin and how Ivory could be beneficial to all three. In 1925, for instance, in the "Beauty Is Fragile" advertisement, the copy discussed what specialists advised for the skin as well as the scientific basis for using soap.[22]

The focus of the advertisements remained the same during the 1930s. In the January 1930 issue of the *Ladies' Home Journal*, the following advertisement was published:

She pays $780 for nice hands—mine cost me next to nothing!

I don't have $780 a year to spend on a maid—like my nice next-door neighbor, Alice G—, who has two cars and never even washes out a handkerchief! My hands are *my* maids, and with a baby and husband to care for, you can imagine how busy they are.

Perhaps you're like me . . . you enjoy tending babies and home. But at a bridge or tea, you don't want your hands to look useful and stodgy. You want them to be ornamental! Don't I know? For the first year after I was married my hands looked like two neglected orphans. And how I sighed over them!

Strangely enough when my baby came I realized what was the trouble. Every day I put her little clothes through Ivory suds. And my hands always felt soothed afterward. (They usually were like graters after my Monday washing with ordinary "kitchen soup.")

So I decided to try Ivory for all my work. And at the end of a week, I felt as if I had a new pair of hands. Don't say hands can't speak! For they were thanking me for changing my dishwashing and cleaning and clothes—washing into gentle Ivory baths!

If you try my plan, as I hope you will, you'll find Ivory is thrifty because it keeps things like new. It doesn't fade colors . . . or rob paint of its gloss . . . or discolor linoleum as strong soaps do.

But I have my best reward when my neighbor drops in for a chat and a cup of fragrant tea. For I can't help noticing then (I'm only human!) that my hands look as carefree as hers!

Catherine Carr Lewis[23]

The block of copy was conversational and informal, but the focus was similar to that of previous advertisements.

In the mid-1930s the company used advertisements that contained large illustrations at the top and small boxed illustrations at the bottom. For the most part, the large illustrations were faces or hands.

The company's position toward advertising was stated in a full-page advertisement that was published in the May 15, 1911, issue of *Saturday Evening Post*:

Advertising has been a factor—an important factor—in the success of Ivory Soap.

But—would you buy Ivory Soap if you could get better soap for the price you pay for Ivory? No!

Would you buy Ivory Soap if you could get another soap, as good as Ivory, for less than you pay for Ivory? Of course not.

Advertising is merely an evidence of a manufacturer's faith in the merit of an article.

Continuous advertising is proof of the public's confidence in it.

Ivory Soap has been advertised, *continuously*, for more than thirty years. [The last paragraph of copy was in smaller-size print:]

For bath, toilet and fine laundry purposes; for the nursery; for shampooing; for everything and anything that necessitates the use of a better-than-ordinary soap, Ivory Soap is unequalled.[24]

The early advertisements for Ivory were successful in generating sales. The various ideas that germinated in Harley Procter's mind were revolutionary in the sense that many had not been attempted by anyone. As Charles Goodrum and Helen Dalrymple pointed out, Harley (1) knew that with the company's white soap he had a specific, identifiable brand; (2) realized that he needed to advertise to consumers—the individuals who purchased products—to explain why the product was better than its competition and to express how the product was beneficial; (3) knew that the product was 99.44 percent pure and therefore could use this fact in the advertisements; (4) realized that the product's strength was its unquestionable value or quality and consequently implied this characteristic or attribute in the advertisements; and (5) knew that advertising to consumers was important, if not crucial, to increasing awareness and sales.[25]

When Harley left the company, the advertisements for Ivory basically remained the same, consistent with those that Harley had created. In short, the advertisements focused on the same characteristics and attributes of the product that Harley thought were important.

NOTES

1. Richard L. Bushman and Claudia L. Bushman, "The Early History of Cleanliness in America," *The Journal of American History*, Vol. 74, No. 4 (March 1988), p. 1215.

2. Ibid., pp. 1220–1221.

3. Ibid., p. 1228.

4. Samuel Colgate, "American Soap Factories," *One Hundred Years of American Commerce: 1795–1895*, vol. 2, ed. Chauncey M. Depew (New York: Greenwood Press, 1968; originally published in 1895), p. 422.

5. Ibid.

6. Ibid., p. 423.

7. Ibid.

8. Horace Greeley et al., *The Great Industries of the United States: Being an Historical Summary of the Origin, Growth and Perfection of the Chief Industrial Arts of this Country* (Hartford, Conn.: J. B. Burr and Hyde, 1872), p. 925.

9. *Cincinnati Gazette*, June 29, 1838.

10. M. Jill Austin and Lynn Brumfield, "P & G's Run-in with the Devil," *Business and Society Review*, No. 78 (Summer 1991); Zachary Schiller, "P & G Is Still Having a Devil of a Time," *Business Week* (September 11, 1995), p. 46.

11. Greeley et al., *The Great Industries of the United States.*

12. Charles Cist, *Sketches and Statistics of Cincinnati in 1859* (Cincinnati: n.p., 1859), p. 266.

13. Ida M. Tarbell, *The Nationalizing of Business 1878–1898* (New York: Macmillan Co., 1936), pp. 174–175.

14. Oscar Schisgall, *Eyes on Tomorrow: The Evolution of Procter & Gamble* (Chicago: J. G. Ferguson Publishing Co., 1981), pp. 133–134.

15. Editors of *Advertising Age. Procter & Gamble: The House That Ivory Built* (Lincolnwood, Ill.: NTC Business Books, 1988), p. 10.

16. *The Independent*, December 21, 1882.

17. *Harper's Weekly* (January 5, 1895).

18. *The Ladies' Home Journal* (May 1896).

19. *The Ladies' Home Journal* (December 1897).

20. *The Ladies' Home Journal* (July 1910).

21. *The Ladies' Home Journal* (May 1915).

22. *The Ladies' Home Journal* (May 1925).

23. *The Ladies' Home Journal* (January 1930).

24. *Saturday Evening Post* (May 15, 1911).

25. Charles Goodrum and Helen Dalrymple, *Advertising in America: The First 200 Years* (New York: Harry N. Abrams, 1990), pp. 51, 54.

8

The Springs Cotton Mills Advertising Campaign of the Late 1940s and Early 1950s

The advertising campaign for the Springs Cotton Mills was one of the most successful advertising campaigns during the late 1940s and early 1950s. It also was one of the most controversial advertising campaigns of these decades. The campaign was created for the Springs Cotton Mills and its Springmaid brand of fabrics and sheets. Sparked by the company's owner, Elliott White Springs, the advertisements in the campaign were controversial because of the language and illustrations, both of which contained or implied sexual connotations. The campaign increased brand awareness and, subsequently, sales.

SEX IN ADVERTISING

Sex has been used by advertisers for years. According to Robert Atwan, Donald McQuade, and John W. Wright, "Sex as a selling tool lies at the core of America's economy of abundance, and advertising has been instrumental in putting it there."[1] However, does sex, whether implied or otherwise, actually help sell a product?

According to John M. Trytten, "[S]ex doesn't sell the product (except for certain specific products)."[2] Furthermore, he claimed that sex did not sell products as well as good stories about those products.[3]

In the study *Fashion and Eroticism: Ideals of Feminine Beauty from the Victorian Era to the Jazz Age,* Valerie Steele discussed Freud's concept of the libido and looking as well as Flugel's concept of women's fashion and eroticism. She wrote:

Women's fashion is said to attract by means of the selective exposure, concealment, and emphasis on the various erotic "zones" of the female body. These can be the secondary sexual characteristics (such as the breasts, hips, and derriere), or parts of the body that acquire sexual connotations (such as the legs, feet, back, waist, shoulders, and so on). According to this theory, male sexual interest in these portions of the anatomy fluctuates, "and it is the business of fashion to pursue [the shifting erogenous zone], without actually catching it up." The fashionable exposure or emphasis must be extreme enough to be exciting, but not so overt as to be widely considered obscene.[4]

Steele claimed that if the body were exposed to view, it would leave nothing to the imagination and consequently would be perceived as ordinary and, eventually, hardly noticed. Thus, she claimed that fashion maintained "erotic interest in the body by ensuring that interesting variations cause the viewer to *see* the body with renewed interest and awareness."[5]

She also discussed the attractiveness of underclothes:

Sensations of softness and warmth and of silky materials gently rubbing against the skin, an intimate connections with the body, a combination of secrecy and visual effect, and a justifiable sense of luxury—a "little fortune"—were all components of lingerie that contributed to reinforcing a sense of femininity.[6]

Elliott White Springs intuitively knew that nudes were not as attractive to the reader as women who were dressed and rationalized that language, if suggestive, would be noticed by women as well as men. Concurrently, he apparently thought that teasing the reader with a provocative illustration and suggestive language rather than with a photograph would have a positive effect.

ELLIOTT WHITE SPRINGS: WHO WAS HE?

Elliott White Springs was born before 1900. He attended Princeton University, from which he graduated in 1917. He enlisted in the U.S. Army and trained as a pursuit pilot. Before World War I ended, he became the third-ranking flying ace by downing 11 German planes. When he returned home he worked as a test pilot; however, when his plane crashed in the first U.S. cross-country race, he gave up flying and went to work for his father, Leroy Springs, who owned several mills in South Carolina.

Springs, who suffered from ulcers, did not enjoy working at the mills. He returned to flying and "buzzed" the mills, which ultimately caused his father to dismiss him. Springs moved to Paris, France, had an operation on his stomach, and started writing wartime aviation novels, including the sardonic *War Birds*, and short stories. The latter were purchased by magazines such as *McClure's*. By the time his father offered him the position of vice president, he had written nine novels and numerous short stories and had earned approximately $250,000.

In 1931 Springs became president and chief executive officer of the company upon his father's death. At the time, the company, which had produced unbranded cotton cloth since its founding in 1888, was worth more than $7 million, with annual sales slightly more than $8 million.[7] Like many businesses, the Springs Cotton Mills suffered during the 1930s as a result of the Great Depression.

Nonetheless, Springs was determined to have fun while managing his business. According to him, presidents of cotton mills could be divided into three classes:

First, there is the Honorable Gentleman. He attends all conventions, sits on the platform at all banquets, and will always agree to shut down for the good of the industry. . . .

Next, there is the Bastard, Second Class. He runs his plant at capacity until his warehouse is full of cloth and his office full of bankers. Then he tries to get rid of them by selling all his goods in one day. . . .

Lastly, there is the Bastard, First Class. He runs his mills twenty-four hours a day, six days in the week, fifty-two weeks in the year. When he goes to New York he lunches alone at the Automat.[8]

Springs considered himself to be in the third category. As president, Springs consolidated the five scattered cotton mills in Fort Mill, Lancaster, Kershaw, and Chester, South Carolina, into the Springs Cotton Mills. Then he applied his creative skills to the Lancaster and Chester Railway, a slightly less than 30-mile line that his father had purchased primarily to ship goods to and from his mills. Springs purchased the private car "Loretto," which had belonged to Charles Schwab before his death, and made the car Lancaster and Chester's regional office. Next, he created a map that contained a network of railroad lines that crisscrossed 15 states and labeled it the "Lancaster & Chester Railway System." He added, in much smaller type, "and connecting lines."[9] Springs had a vice president for every mile of track. The vice presidents were personal friends who were prosperous in other endeavors. This humorous marketing concept helped the small railway earn a profit every year thereafter.

Springs, unlike some other presidents of cotton mills, never closed one mill during the Great Depression. When World War II erupted, the Springs Cotton Mills filled orders for the War Protection Board and earned the coveted Army and Navy "E" Award for excellent performance on war contracts.[10] According to Springs, the Japanese could detect ordinary camouflage cloth because of its lack of endemic odors. Thus, his company perfected a process in which camouflage cloth was impregnated with the scent of the jungle. The company produced other types of cloth with special characteristics for the War Production Board.

Before the war ended, Springs had prepared his company to become a major marketer of consumer goods by differentiating his finished cotton products through branding and advertising under the Springmaid label. In addition to building a cotton finishing plant, a foundry, and another facility to test various fabrics, processes, and equipment, he opened Springs Mills, Inc., in New York in 1945, primarily to sell Springmaid products. Prior to this year the company's products had been sold through other companies in New York.[11]

Springs started advertising Springmaid products the same year. He became disillusioned with the advertising campaign within a year. For instance, in 1946 he wrote to the Gatch Advertising Agency, which had created the campaign: "Your advertising campaign needs pepping up. We have had too many pictures of horses with some very tiresome text underneath to prove, in six paragraphs, that the horses are thoroughbreds, and so are our sheets."[12]

In the same letter, Springs criticized the agency's campaign and other advertising campaigns, claiming, "Many advertisements are an insult to second grade IQ and are just as dull as yours."[13] Then he explained several advertisements that should be considered by the agency. The first depicted a girl on a street corner with the wind blowing her skirt. The copy explained that the company had developed a special cotton fabric that was windproof. The second depicted a girl striking a match on the seat of her pants. The copy explained that the company had developed a special cotton fabric for the abrasive trade. The third depicted a girl being pinched at a party. The copy explained that the company had developed a crease-proof cotton fabric.

Springs requested that the agency have an artist create a series of subtle, sexy advertisements that incorporated illustrations, not photographs. Although the agency attempted to please Springs, the artist's sketches were rejected, as the following excerpt from a letter illustrates:

What I wanted was a subtle picture of a girl with her skirt agitated by the wind.

You send me down a picture of a girl standing over an air jet with her skirts blown over her head like Coney Island! It's about as subtle as the Can Can.[14]

The agency's artist returned to the drawing board; however, upon receiving the sketches, Springs reiterated what he had emphasized in his previous letter. The Gatch Advertising Agency failed in its efforts, and Springs searched for other advertising agencies, without success. Eventually, he procured illustrations from several artists and wrote the accompanying copy. The new advertising campaign, which was handled by Hill Wolfe, the head of the company's advertising department in New York, and the advertising agency Erwin, Wasey and Company began in May 1948 in several magazines, including *Charm, Cue, Esquire, Fortune, Holiday, The New York Times Magazine,* and the *Saturday Evening Post.*

THE CAMPAIGN AND ITS REPERCUSSIONS

Within two months the campaign's purpose was discussed in *Tide*, a trade publication: "The general idea of this activity is to get positive national identification for the traditional Springmaid label. There are, however, a number of secondary ideas. The principal one, as the company puts it, is to 'liven up' textile advertising."[15]

The writer of the article mentioned that there were at least three versions of a particular advertisement because of the copy:

The copy is so unusual that the agency has made it permanent operating procedure to check every word with the magazine involved before the insertion contract is drawn up. Where it feels that a publisher's squeamishness is justified, or when it particularly wants to get the copy in, the agency makes required alterations.[16]

The campaign and its creator were also discussed in several mass-circulated magazines, including *Time*. This publicity helped stimulate interest among certain members of the press and, more important, among readers.

One of the first advertisements in the campaign depicted a young, attractive woman ice-skating with one leg up in the air; her panties were exposed to the reader and to two elderly gentlemen seated on a bench. The headline "Pungent Paragraphs" introduced four paragraphs of copy:

During the war, The Springs Cotton Mills was called upon to develop a special fabric for camouflage. It was used in the Pacific to conceal ammunition dumps and gun emplacements, but the Japanese learned to detect it because of its lack of jungle smells.

To overcome this, when the fabric was dyed, it was also impregnated with a permanent odor of hibiscus, hydranges, and old rubber boots. The deception was so successful that when Tokyo fell, the victorious invaders hung a piece of this fabric on a Japanese flagpole.

This process has been patented, and the fabric is now available to the false bottom and bust bucket business as SPRINGMAID *PERKER*, made of combed yarns, 37" wide, 152 × 68 approximate count, weight about 3.30, the white with gardenia, the pink with camellia, the blush with jasmine, and the nude dusty.

If you want to achieve that careless look and avoid skater's steam, kill two birds with one stone by getting a camouflaged callipygian camisole with the SPRINGMAID label on the bottom of your trademark.[17]

The words "false bottom" and "bust bucket" certainly would be offensive to many women and to certain editors of trade papers that critique advertisements.

Just as in every advertisement in the campaign, the advertisement contained the name and address of the manufacturer as well as the Springmaid logo.

Another early advertisement in the campaign depicted a young, attractive woman standing barefoot in a puddle of water. Wearing a halter top and a short skirt that has been blown by the wind, she has tossed leaves of various colors about her. The headline "Be Protected" introduced two paragraphs of copy:

During the war, the Springs Cotton Mills was called upon to develop a crease-proof cotton fabric. It was used with great success as a backing for maps, photographs, and other valuable assets. This fabric has now been further perfected and made available to the torso-twister trade.

After a convention, a clam-bake, or a day in the Pentagon Building, you need not eat off the mantel if you have your foundation covered with SPRINGMAID *POKER* woven of combed yarns 37" wide, 152 × 68 count, in tearose, white, nude, and black, light and medium gauge. If you bruise easily, you can face the future confidently with the SPRINGMAID trademark.[18]

Although the copy may not have been offensive, the illustration, because it revealed the young, attractive woman's panties, may have offended some readers, especially those readers of some of the magazines in which the advertisement appeared; the advertisement appeared in magazines that were read by women.

Another early advertisement in the campaign depicted a young, attractive woman dressed in a tied blouse and a revealing skirt skipping rope. The headline "Fortify Your Foundations" introduced one paragraph of copy that had been excerpted from an article. The article had appeared in *The Bawl Street Journal*. The paragraph read:

One of the most interesting sets of questionnaires came from Congress. So far, he said, he has been unable to fit this group into any previously known category. He sounded a note of warning to young females, however, saying his researches indicated that any such person subject to bruises should wear at least two thicknesses of girdles before venturing on Capitol Hill. A chest protector would also be valuable in a pinch, he added.[19]

Such a publication did not exist. Again, Springs was having fun with the copy, as the excerpt illustrates.

Another early advertisement in the campaign also featured the excerpt from the article that had appeared in *The Bawl Street Journal*. The illustration featured a young, attractive woman standing in water. She had a surprised expression on her face, which was caused by one large duck and two small ducks swimming nearby. The young woman had pulled up her dress. Of course, her panties were revealed to the reader. The headline "Beware the Goose!" playfully introduced three paragraphs of copy, which, for the most part, described the company's cotton fabric. The words "hip harness" and "bosom bolster" were used to identify certain prospective businesses.[20]

Another advertisement contained two paragraphs of copy that rhymed. The illustration depicted an early American military officer with a sword on his hip and a young, attractive housekeeper or maid in a bedroom. An older man could be seen through the opened bedroom door; he was standing on stair steps peering in. The headline "Bundling without Bungling" introduced the copy:

When knightly bundling was in flower and great-grandpa was in his bower, he often played heck with a sheet for he slept with spurs upon his feet. And when a nightmare made him twitch, the damsel really had to stitch. But both the sheets and great-grandma survived the calls of great-grandpa. Since boots and spurs are not in vogue and guest rooms are today the mode, your sheets must still stand rips and tears of laundries, kids, and derrieres. But mending sheets is now passe; our whistle bait has a better way, and sheets don't face such knightly slaughter. A colonial dame's great-granddaughter selects our own FORT SUMTER sheets to spur beaux on to spurless feats.

Unlike old times when couples bundled and in the process often bungled, we make our SPRINGMAIDS much the best and proved it in a strenuous test. We took our own FORT SUMTER brand, woven and finished by skillful hand. Each sheet was washed 400 times—a test like this would slick new dimes. Two hundred times they were abraded, yet none were either worn or faded. That's equal to a generation of wear and tear and vellication. In speaking of FORT SUMTER covers, we really wish all fabric lovers, when homeward bound from some dull party, would test SPRINGMAIDS—they're all so hardy that you can get a running start and dive in—they won't come apart. The moral is, to each of you: No matter what you say or do, remember that in cold or heat, you can't go wrong on a SPRINGMAID sheet.[21]

The copy has more than one inference, which was, of course, the writer's intention. In short, the advertisement was selling more than sheets; it was promoting sexual intercourse.

Another advertisement in the campaign had an illustration that depicted three cheerleaders jumping in front of a crowd of spectators. The headline "Safe in the End Zone" introduced two paragraphs of copy, which concerned "Mediker," a special fabric that was developed during World War II for the medical department. The copy claimed that the fabric was useful for self-applied bandages.[22]

In another advertisement, the illustration depicted a young, attractive woman carrying two bags of groceries; however, she was having difficulty walking because her panties had fallen to her ankles. The headline "Watch the Butter Fly" introduced three paragraphs of copy, which discussed the "Sticker," a special cotton fabric that contained rubber. Actually developed for hospital use, the product was being offered to makers of underwear. The copy also mentioned the cloth's measurements and colors. The advertisement's last two paragraphs read:

Don't depend on buttons and bows, but switch to *STICKER* and let the SPRINGMAID label protect you from the consequences of embarrassing accidents such as pictured above.

We stick behind our fabric and feel its tenacity so strongly that we call it an insurance policy to provide full coverage. Our only competition comes from a tattoo artist.[23]

Several advertisements were developed for the company's sheets. One of the first advertisements had an illustration of a young, attractive woman who had leaped from a window of a burning building. Four firemen, holding a sheet, were going to catch her. However, they were smiling at the woman in distress; her dress had been blown to her waist. Her panties and stockings were visible to the firemen and to the reader. The headline "We Love to Catch Them on a Springmaid Sheet" introduced four paragraphs of copy that discussed the quality and durability of the company's sheets.[24]

Another advertisement depicted an early American military officer escaping from an upstairs window. A young, attractive woman the officer had been visiting appeared distressed as her apparent grandfather was about to cut the sheet by which the officer was escaping. The headline "Bungled Bundling" introduced two paragraphs of copy; the first paragraph:

In olden times throughout this land our maidens made their sheets by hand. They used a spinning wheel until it was replaced by cotton mill. Then, lovers found more than one use for strong sheets that could stand abuse. They used them to avoid grandsire and thereby to escape his ire. Our knight slid often down a sheet with eyes on girl and spurs on feet. But sometimes luck just wasn't there when grandpa's hatchet cut through air. Today we weave FORT SUMTER sheets in such a way that always meets with every family's bedroom need from restful sleep to militant deed.[25]

The remaining paragraph, also in rhyme, explained the strenuous test that was applied to Springmaid sheets.

In another advertisement for Springmaid sheets, the illustration depicted a young, attractive Indian squaw and a young Indian chief in a hammock made from a sheet. The chief appeared exhausted, and the attractive squaw appeared happy; the illustration suggested that the chief and the squaw had just had sexual intercourse. The headline "A buck well spent on a Springmaid Sheet" introduced three paragraphs of copy that discussed the quality and durability of the company's sheets.[26]

Springs used sex primarily to capture the reader's attention, then used double entendre or puns to tease and inform the reader about Springmaid products. The feminine figures that dominated the advertisements were often leggy and shown in unusual situations. The figures captured the reader's attention and invariably forced him or her to not only glance at the head-line but read the copy. Concurrently, the company's logo was prominently displayed.

The copy in these and other advertisements in the campaign was soon scrutinized by several trade publications. For instance, in the August 27, 1948, issue of *Tide*, the copy was considered "ribald" and ineffective, as the following excerpt illustrates:

Its copy in consumer magazines has astonished a rather large number of people in and out of advertising by its disarming use, in describing articles of female underclothing, of expressions like "false bottom and bust bucket," "ham hamper and lung lifter," "hip harness and bosom bolster."[27]

According to the article, "Agency men who have seen the copy are most upset (90%) by it; advertisers are two-to-one against it."[28]

As if criticism by certain trade publications had not been enough, several magazines refused to run the advertisements al-together because of phrases such as "ham hamper," "lung lifter," and "rumba aroma." Newspapers, on the other hand, seemed less concerned about the copy. According to Springs, the *New York Times*, the *New York Herald Tribune*, and several others accepted the advertisements without any changes in the art or the copy.[29]

In the September 10, 1948, issue of *Tide*, the controversy sur-rounding the campaign was discussed by Charlotte Montgom-ery, who explained the advertisements—that is, the illustrations ("semi-nudes") and the copy ("baffling"), then asked whether the advertisements were directed to consumers. Finally, she ed-itorialized about the campaign:

I feel mighty cynical about the whole thing. I wonder if someone is using a very expensive method to amuse his friends, collect pictures for his whoopie room and cause talk that may flatter egos but can do more harm than good in the long run.[30]

The writer of this column was not alone in her criticism. Springs received numerous letters from readers who had read

the advertisements, and many complained, as the following excerpt illustrates: "Your illustrations and copy are both vulgar—
and I feel, as do many with whom I have spoken—that you are
certainly doing yourself more harm than good."[31]

In the December 3, 1948, issue of *Printers' Ink*, the writer of the
column "Aesop Glim's Clinic" discussed truth as well as good
taste in advertising. According to the writer, advertising needed
both, primarily to improve its image in the public's mind. Then
the writer added:

As a flagrant, current example of bad taste we have with us today . . .
the Springmaid Fabrics campaign. . . . The advertisements Aesop Glim
has seen have all been in "general public" media. If this means they are
addressed to women, he is reasonably sure they don't speak the language—in either picture or word. . . .
   Finally, if these advertisements are really addressed to the garment
industry, they're in the wrong publications.[32]

In the December 10, 1948, issue of *Printers' Ink*, the president
and publisher of the magazine condemned the controversial
campaign in his column "The Publisher Speaks":

The only thing that worries me is that the advertiser himself and some
others will be deceived by the fact that his campaign is talked about.
They will dig up the old chestnut about "Better to be talked about badly
than not talked about at all." We may see a slight epidemic of double-
entendre advertising. And that, I think, would be bad for the cause of
advertising as a whole.[33]

Roland Smith, a professor of advertising at the time, criticized
the campaign in the article "After Hours: Publicity Isn't Advertising," which appeared in the December 17, 1948, issue of *Printers' Ink*:

Since when did publicity—bad publicity at that—take the place of com-
petent advertising, or begin substituting for it? . . .
   It seems to me that Springs Mills is making enemies for its products
as rapidly as it's making a few friends.[34]

As the controversial campaign was discussed by members of
the press, it became increasingly popular. Before 1949, for in-

stance, Springs was receiving approximately 50 letters a day. According to him, 98 percent of the letters were favorable toward the campaign.[35] In addition, the advertisements had appeared in the following magazines: *American Magazine, Charm, Collier's, Coronet, Cosmopolitan, Cue, Esquire, Fortune, Harper's Magazine, Holiday, Hotel Management, Life, Look, Mademoiselle, Newsweek, New Yorker, The Pathfinder, Promenade, Pic, South Carolina Magazine, Saturday Evening Post, Southern Agriculturist, Town and Country, Time,* and *Vogue,* which indicated that publishers, even some who had rejected the advertisements initially, had grown more tolerant toward the illustrations and copy or that the agency had been successful in responding to certain requests, as mentioned.

THE RESULTS OF THE CAMPAIGN

The advertisements for this particular campaign appeared in magazines through 1951. In that period—1948–1951—Starch readership surveys revealed greater copy recall and greater brand recognition for Springs' advertisements than for any other campaign.[36] Thus, Springs had accomplished one objective: national brand name awareness. However, sales of products with the Springmaid label also increased. In 1948, for instance, sales were about $105 million. By the end of 1951, sales had increased to approximately $120 million. In 1959, when Springs died, and executives of the company decided to discontinue his humorous style of advertising, sales had increased to $170 million. The company had become one of the largest makers of sheets.[37]

The use of attractive figures depicted in unusual situations had been productive. Not only had Springmaid become a household name, but the company's products sold extremely well. The advertising had been effective no matter what the pundits claimed.

NOTES

1. Robert Atwant, Donald McQuade, and John W. Wright, *Edsels, Luckies, and Frigidaires: Advertising the American Way* (New York: Dell Publishing Co., 1979), p. 326.

2. John M. Trytten, "Sex in Advertising: The Easy Way Out!" *Sales Management* (May 28, 1973), p. 36.

3. Ibid.

4. Valerie Steele, *Fashion and Eroticism: Ideals of Feminine Beauty from the Victorian Era to the Jazz Age* (New York: Oxford University Press, 1985), p. 34.

5. Ibid., p. 42.

6. Ibid., p. 208.

7. *The Story of the Springs Cotton Mills: 1888–1963* (Fort Mill, S.C.: Springs Mills, 1963), n.p.

8. "Playboy of the Textile World," *Fortune* (January 1950), p. 66.

9. "Textile Tempest," *Time* (July 26, 1948), p. 72.

10. *The Story of the Springs Cotton Mills.*

11. Ibid.

12. Elliott White Springs, *Clothes Make the Man* (New York: J. J. Little and Ives Co., 1949), p. 84.

13. Ibid., p. 85.

14. Ibid., p. 90.

15. "Springmaid," *Tide* (July 16, 1948); reprinted in Springs, *Clothes Make the Man*, p. 120.

16. Ibid.

17. *Coronet* (August 1948).

18. *Coronet* (November 1948).

19. *Coronet* (December 1948).

20. *Coronet* (February 1949).

21. *Coronet* (June 1949).

22. *Coronet* (August 1949).

23. *Coronet* (December 1949).

24. *Coronet* (February 1950).

25. *Coronet* (April 1950).

26. *Coronet* (June 1950).

27. "Tide Leadership Survey," *Tide* (August 27, 1948), p. 53.

28. Ibid.

29. Springs, *Clothes Make the Man*, p. 228.

30. Charlotte Montgomery, "The Woman's Viewpoint," *Tide* (September 10, 1948), p. 24.

31. Springs, *Clothes Make the Man*, p. 137.

32. "Aesop Glim's Clinic," *Printers' Ink* (December 3, 1948), p. 75.

33. C. B. Larrabee, "The Publisher Speaks: Bad Taste Leaves a Bad Taste," *Printers' Ink* (December 10, 1948), p. 5.

34. Roland B. Smith, "After Hours: Publicity Isn't Advertising," *Printers' Ink* (December 17, 1948), p. 124.

35. Springs, *Clothes Make the Man*, p. 152.

36. Charles Goodrum and Helen Dalrymple, *Advertising in America: The First 200 Years* (New York: Harry N. Abrams, 1990), p. 77.

37. *The Story of the Springs Cotton Mills*.

Bibliography

BOOKS

Albion, Robert G. *The Rise of New York Port*. New York: Charles Scribner's Sons, 1939.

Allen, James Sloan. *The Romance of Commerce and Culture: Capitalism, Modernism, and the Chicago-Aspen Crusade for Cultural Reform*. Chicago and London: University of Chicago Press, 1983.

Atwan, Robert, Donald McQuade, and John W. Wright. *Edsels, Luckies, and Frigidaires: Advertising the American Way*. New York: Dell Publishing Co., 1979.

Barnum, P. T. *Barnum's Own Story: The Autobiography of P. T. Barnum*. New York: Dover Publications, 1961.

———. *Struggles and Triumphs or, Forty Years' Recollections of P. T. Barnum*, with introduction by Roy F. Dibble. New York: Macmillan Co., 1930.

Bleyer, Willard G. *Main Currents in the History of American Journalism*. Boston: Houghton Mifflin Co., 1927.

Blum, John M., Edmund S. Morgan, Willie Lee Rose, Arthur M. Schlesinger, Jr., Kenneth M. Stampp, and C. Vann Woodward. *The National Experience*. New York: Harcourt Brace Jovanovich, 1981.

Boorstin, Daniel J. *The Americans: The Colonial Experience*. New York: Random House, 1958.

———. *The Americans: The Democratic Experience*. New York: Random House, 1973.

———. *The Americans: The National Experience*. New York: Random House, 1965.

————. *The Image or What Happened to the American Dream.* New York: Atheneum, 1962.

Bradford, Gamaliel. *Damaged Souls.* Boston: Houghton Mifflin Co., 1931.

Bridenbaugh, Carl A. *Cities in the Wilderness.* New York: Ronald Press Co., 1938.

Brigham, Clarence S. *Journals and Journeymen: A Contribution to the History of Early American Newspapers.* Philadelphia: University of Pennsylvania Press, 1950.

Broune, Waldo R., ed. *Barnum's Own Story: The Autobiography of P. T. Barnum.* New York: Dover Publications, 1961.

Bryan, J., III. *The World's Greatest Showman: The Life of P. T. Barnum.* New York: Random House, 1956.

Cahn, William. *Out of the Cracker Barrel: The Nabisco Story from Animal Crackers to Zuzus.* New York: Simon and Schuster, 1969.

Carson, Gerald. *The Old Country Store.* New York: Oxford University Press, 1954.

Cist, Charles. *Sketches and Statistics of Cincinnati in 1859.* Cincinnati: n.p., listed, 1859.

Clark, Victor S. *History of Manufactures in the United States, 1697–1860.* Washington, D.C.: Carnegie Institution, 1916.

Cleary, David Powers. *Great American Brands: The Successful Formulas That Made Them Famous.* New York: Fairchild Publications, 1981.

Cole, Arthur H. *The American Wool Manufacturer.* Cambridge: Harvard University Press, 1926.

Cone, Fairfax M. *With All Its Faults.* Boston: Little, Brown and Co., 1969.

Cook, Elizabeth Christine. *Literary Influences in Colonial Newspapers— 1704–1750.* New York: Columbia University Press, 1912.

Cook, James. *Remedies and Rackets: The Truth about Patent Medicines Today,* with an introduction by Oliver Field. New York: W. W. Norton and Co., 1958.

Courtney, Alice E., and Thomas W. Whipple. *Sex Stereotyping in Advertising.* Lexington, Mass.: Lexington Books, 1983.

Cramp, Arthur J., ed. *Nostrums and Quackery.* Vol. 2. Chicago: American Medical Association, 1921.

Depew, Chauncey M., ed. *One Hundred Years of American Commerce: 1795–1895.* Vol. 2. New York: D. O. Haynes and Co., 1895; New York: Greenwood Press, 1968.

Dill, William A. *Growth of Newspapers in the United States.* Lawrence: Department of Journalism, University of Kansas, 1928.

Editors of *Advertising Age. How It Was in Advertising: 1776–1976.* Chicago: Crain Books, 1976.

————. *Procter & Gamble: The House That Ivory Built.* Lincolnwood, Ill.: NTC Business Books, 1988.

Emery, Michael, and Edwin Emery. *The Press and America: An Interpretive History of the Mass Media.* Englewood Cliffs, N.J.: Prentice-Hall, 1988.

Ferry, John William. *A History of the Department Store.* New York: Macmillan Co., 1960.

Filler, Louis. *Appointment at Armageddon: Muckraking and Progressivism in the American Tradition.* Westport, Conn.: Greenwood Press, 1976.

Folkerts, Jean, and Dwight L. Teeter, Jr. *Voices of a Nation: A History of Media in the United States.* New York: Macmillan Publishing Co., 1989.

Fox, Stephen. *The Mirror Makers: A History of American Advertising and Its Creators.* New York: William Morrow and Co., 1984.

Gibbons, Herbert Adams. *John Wanamaker.* 2 vols. Port Washington, N.Y.: Kennikat Press, 1971; originally published in 1926.

Giesecke, Albert A. *American Commercial Legislation before 1789.* Philadelphia: University of Pennsylvania Press, 1910.

Glynn, Prudence. *Skin to Skin: Eroticism in Dress.* New York: Oxford University Press, 1982.

Goodrum, Charles, and Helen Dalrymple. *Advertising in America: The First 200 Years.* New York: Harry N. Abrams, 1990.

Gray, Lewis C. *History of Agriculture in the Southern United States to 1860.* Vol. 1. Washington, D.C.: Carnegie Institution, 1933.

Greeley, Horace, et al. *The Great Industries of the United States: Being an Historical Summary of the Origin, Growth and Perfection of the Chief Industrial Arts of This Country.* Hartford, Conn.: J. B. Burr and Hyde, 1872.

Gunther, John. *Taken at the Flood: The Story of Albert D. Lasker.* New York: Harper and Brothers, 1960.

Haller, John S. *American Medicine in Transition: 1840–1910.* Urbana: University of Illinois Press, 1981.

Harrington, Virginia D. *The New York Merchant on the Eve of the Revolution.* New York: Columbia University Press, 1935.

Harris, Neil. *Cultural Excursions: Marketing Appetites and Cultural Tastes in Modern America.* Chicago and London: University of Chicago Press, 1990.

————. *Humbug: The Art of P. T. Barnum.* Boston: Little, Brown and Co., 1973.

Heilbroner, Robert L., and Aaron Singer. *The Economic Transformation of*

America: 1600 to the Present. 2d ed. New York: Harcourt Brace Jovanovich, 1984.

Hopkins, Claude C. *My Life in Advertising.* New York: Harper and Brothers, 1927.

Hower, Ralph M. *The History of an Advertising Agency: N. W. Ayer and Son at Work, 1869–1949.* Cambridge: Harvard University Press, 1949.

Hubbard, Elbert. *Lydia E. Pinkham: Being a Sketch of Her Life and Times.* East Aurora, N.Y.: Roycrofters, 1915.

Hudson, Frederic. *Journalism in the United States from 1690 to 1872.* New York: Harper and Brothers, 1873.

Ingham, John N. *Biographical Dictionary of American Business Leaders: A–G.* Westport, Conn.: Greenwood Press, 1983.

———. *Biographical Dictionary of American Business Leaders: V–Z.* Westport, Conn.: Greenwood Press, 1983.

Johnson, Allen, ed. *Dictionary of American Biography, Vol. 1 Abbe-Brazer.* New York: Charles Scribner's Sons, 1927.

Johnson, E. R., T. W. Van Metre, G. G. Huebner, and D. S. Hanchett. *History of Domestic and Foreign Commerce of the United States.* Vol. 1. Washington, D.C.: Carnegie Institution, 1915.

Jones, Fred M. *Middlemen in the Domestic Trade of the United States, 1800–1860.* Urbana: University of Illinois Press, 1937.

Jones, Robert W. *Journalism in the United States.* New York: E. P. Dutton and Co., 1947.

Kirkland, Edward C. *A History of American Economic Life.* 3d ed. New York: Appleton-Century-Crofts, 1951.

Knowlton, Evelyn H. *Pepperell's Progress.* Cambridge: Harvard University Press, 1948.

Kobre, Sidney. *Development of American Journalism.* Dubuque, Iowa: William C. Brown Co., 1969.

———. *The Development of the Colonial Newspaper.* Gloucester, Mass.: Peter Smith, 1960.

Labaree, Leonard W., Ralph L. Ketchum, Helen C. Boatfield, and Helen H. Fineman, eds. *The Autobiography of Benjamin Franklin* by Benjamin Franklin. New Haven, Conn.: Yale University Press, 1964.

Labaree, Leonard W., and Whitfield J. Bell, Jr., eds. *The Papers of Benjamin Franklin, Vol. 3: January 1, 1745, through June 30, 1750.* New Haven: Yale University Press, 1961.

Lasker, Albert D. *The Lasker Story . . . As He Told It.* Chicago: Advertising Publications, 1963.

Leach, William. *Land of Desire: Merchants, Power, and the Rise of a New American Culture.* New York: Pantheon Books, 1993.

Lears, Jackson. *Fables of Abundance: A Cultural History of Advertising in America*. New York: Basic Books, 1994.

Lee, Alfred M. *The Daily Newspaper in America: The Evolution of a Social Instrument*. New York: Macmillan Co., 1947.

Lee, James M. *History of American Journalism*. Garden City, N.Y.: Garden City Publishing Co., 1917.

Lemay, J. A. Leo, and P. M. Zall, eds. *The Autobiography of Benjamin Franklin: A Genetic Text*. Knoxville: University of Tennessee Press, 1981.

Malone, Dumas, ed. *Dictionary of American Biography: Vol. 8, Platt-Seward*. New York: Charles Scribner's Sons, 1935.

Marchand, Roland. *Advertising the American Dream: Making Way for Modernity, 1920–1940*. Berkeley and Los Angeles: University of California Press, 1985.

Margolin, Victor, Ira Brichta, and Vivian Brichta. *The Promise and the Product: 200 Years of American Advertising Posters*. New York: Macmillan Publishing Co., 1979.

McNamara, Brooks. *Step Right Up*. Garden City, N.Y.: Doubleday and Co., 1976.

Miller, Michael B. *The Bon Marche: Bourgeois Culture and the Department Store, 1869–1920*. Princeton, N.J.: Princeton University Press, 1981.

Mott, Frank Luther. *American Journalism: A History: 1690–1960*. 3d ed. New York: Macmillan Co., 1962.

———. *A History of American Magazines, Vol. 1: 1741–1850*. New York: D. Appleton and Co., 1930.

The National Cyclopaedia of American Biography. Vol. 20. New York: James T. White and Co., 1929.

The National Cyclopaedia of American Biography. Vol. 2. New York: James T. White and Co., 1921.

Norris, James D. *Advertising and the Transformation of American Society, 1865–1920*. New York: Greenwood Press, 1990.

Pope, Daniel. *The Making of Modern Advertising*. New York: Basic Books, Inc., 1983.

Presbrey, Frank. *The History and Development of Advertising*. Garden City, N.Y.: Doubleday & Co., 1929.

Reilly, Philip J. *Old Masters of Retailing*. New York: Fairchild Publications, 1966.

Richardson, Lyon N. *A History of Early American Magazines 1741–1789*. New York: Octagon Books, 1966; originally published by Thomas Nelson and Sons in 1931.

Robert, Joseph C. *The Tobacco Kingdom: Plantation, Market and Factory in Virginia and North Carolina, 1800–1860.* Durham, N.C.: Duke University Press, 1938.

Root, Harvey W. *The Unknown Barnum.* New York: Harper and Brothers, 1927.

Rowell, George P. *Forty Years an Advertising Agent: 1865–1905.* New York: Printers' Ink Publishing Co., 1906; New York: Garland Publishing, 1985.

———. *The Men Who Advertise.* New York: N. Chesman, 1870.

Rowsome, Frank, Jr. *They Laughed When I Sat Down: An Informal History of Advertising in Words and Pictures.* New York: McGraw-Hill Book Co., 1959.

Saxon, A. H., ed. *Selected Letters of P. T. Barnum.* New York: Columbia University Press, 1983.

Schisgall, Oscar. *Eyes on Tomorrow: The Evolution of Procter & Gamble.* Chicago: J. G. Ferguson Publishing Co., 1981.

Seitz, Don C. *The James Gordon Bennetts: Father and Son: Proprietors of the New York Herald.* Indianapolis: Bobbs-Merrill Co., 1928.

Sellers, Leila. *Charleston Business on the Eve of the American Revolution.* Chapel Hill: University of North Carolina Press, 1934.

Smyth, Albert H. *The Philadelphia Magazines and Their Contributors 1741–1850.* Freeport, N.Y.: Books for Libraries Press, 1970; originally published in 1892.

Springs, Elliott White. *Clothes Make the Man.* New York: J. J. Little and Ives Co., 1949.

Stage, Sarah. *Female Complaints: Lydia Pinkham and the Business of Women's Medicine.* New York: W. W. Norton & Co., 1979.

Steele, Valerie. *Fashion and Eroticism: Ideals of Feminine Beauty from the Victorian Era to the Jazz Age.* New York: Oxford University Press, 1985.

The Story of the Springs Cotton Mills: 1888–1963. Fort Mill, S.C.: Springs Mills, 1963.

Sullivan, Mark. *The Education of an American.* New York: Doubleday, Doran and Co., Inc., 1938.

Tarbell, Ida M. *The Nationalizing of Business 1878–1898.* New York: Macmillan Co., 1936.

Taylor, George Rogers. *The Transportation Revolution, 1815–1860.* New York: Holt, Rinehart and Winston, 1951.

Tebbel, John, and Mary Ellen Zuckerman. *The Magazine in America 1741–1990.* New York: Oxford University Press, 1991.

Thomas, Henry, and Dana Lee Thomas. *50 Great Americans: Their In-*

spiring Lives and Achievements. Garden City, N.Y.: Doubleday and Co., 1948.

Thomas, Isaiah. *The History of Printing in America, with a Biography of Printers in Two Volumes.* 2d ed. New York: Burt Franklin, n.d.; originally published in 1874.

Turner, E. S. *The Shocking History of Advertising.* New York: E. P. Dutton and Co., 1953.

V. B. Palmer's Business-Men's Almanac. New York: V. B. Palmer, 1850.

Vinikas, Vincent. *Soft Soap, Hard Sell: American Hygiene in an Age of Advertisement.* Ames: Iowa State University Press, 1992.

Wallace, Irving. *The Fabulous Showman: The Life and Times of P. T. Barnum.* New York: Alfred A. Knopf, 1959.

Ware, W. Porter, and Thaddeus C. Lockard, Jr. *P. T. Barnum Presents Jenny Lind.* Baton Rouge: Louisiana State University Press, 1980.

Washburn, Robert Collyer. *Life and Times of Lydia Pinkham.* New York: G. P. Putnam's Sons, 1931.

Werner, M. R. *Barnum.* New York: Harcourt, Brace and Co., 1923.

Winthrop, John. *The History of New England from 1630 to 1649.* Vol. 1. Boston: Phelps and Farmham, 1825.

Wood, James Playsted. *Magazines in the United States.* 3d ed. New York: Ronald Press Co., 1971.

———. *The Story of Advertising.* New York: Ronald Press Co., 1958.

Wright, Louis B. *The Cultural Life of the American Colonies 1607–1763.* New York: Harper and Brothers, 1957.

Young, James Harvey. *The Toadstool Millionaires: A Social History of Patent Medicines in America before Federal Regulation.* Princeton, N.J.: Princeton University Press, 1961.

CHAPTERS FROM BOOKS

Applegate, Edd. "Albert D. Lasker (May 1, 1880–May 30, 1952)." *The Ad Men and Women: A Biographical Dictionary of Advertising,* edited by Edd Applegate. Westport, Conn., and London: Greenwood Press, 1994.

Ayer, F. W. "Chapter XIII: Advertising in America." *One Hundred Years of American Commerce: 1795–1895,* vol. 1, edited by Chauncey M. Depew. New York: D. O. Haynes and Co., 1895; New York: Greenwood Press, 1968.

Colgate, Samuel. "Chapter LXII: American Soap Factories." *One Hundred Years of American Commerce: 1795–1895,* vol. 2, edited by Chauncey M. Depew. New York: D. O. Haynes and Co., 1895; New York: Greenwood Press, 1968.

Franklin, Benjamin. "Advice to a Young Tradesman, Written by an Old One. To my Friend A. B." *The Instructor: or Young Man's Best Companion*, edited by George Fisher. Philadelphia: B. Franklin and D. Hall, 1748.

McQuade, Donald A., and Elizabeth Williamson. "Advertising." *Handbook of American Popular Culture Second Edition, Revised and Enlarged Advertising-Graffiti*, edited by M. Thomas Inge. Westport, Conn.: Greenwood Press, 1989.

Smythe, Ted Curtis. "George Prebury Rowell (July 4, 1838–August 28, 1908)." *The Ad Men and Women: A Biographical Dictionary of Advertising*, edited by Edd Applegate. Westport, Conn., and London: Greenwood Press, 1994.

Vannatta, Bonnie. "Volney B. Palmer (1799–July 29, 1864)." *The Ad Men and Women: A Biographical Dictionary of Advertising*, edited by Edd Applegate. Westport, Conn., and London: Greenwood Press, 1994.

Vivian, John. "Francis Wayland Ayer (February 4, 1848–March 5, 1923)." *The Ad Men and Women: A Biographical Dictionary of Advertising*, edited by Edd Applegate. Westport, Conn., and London: Greenwood Press, 1994.

MONOGRAPHS

Holland, Donald R. "Volney B. Palmer (1799–1864): The Nation's First Advertising Agency Man." Lexington, Ky.: Association for Education in Journalism, 1976.

Lasker, Albert D. "Reminiscences." Columbia Oral History Collection, 1949–1950.

PROCEEDINGS

Clark, Charles E. "The Newspapers of Provincial America." *Proceedings of the American Antiquarian Society*. Vol. 100. Worcester, Mass.: American Antiquarian Society, 1990.

ARTICLES

"A. D. Lasker Dies; Philanthropist, 71." *New York Times*, May 31, 1952.

"Advertising: Textile Tempest." *Time* (July 26, 1948).

"Aesop Glim's Clinic." *Printers' Ink* (December 3, 1948).

American Newspaper Reporter (November 20, 1871).

Atherton, Lewis E. "The Pioneer Merchant in Mid-America." *University of Missouri Studies*, Vol. 14 (April 1939).

Austin, M. Jill, and Lynn Brumfield. "P & G's Run-In with the Devil." *Business and Society Review*, No. 78 (Summer 1991).

"Bad Taste Leaves a Bad Taste." *Printers' Ink* (December 10, 1948).

Barbour, C. A. "F. W. Ayer: An Appreciation." *Watchman Examiner*, March 22, 1923.

"Barnum and Advertising." *Printers' Ink* (July 14, 1910).

"Barnum on Top as Usual." *New York Times*, November 22, 1887.

"Barnum's American Museum Burns." *New York Times*, July 14, 1865.

Bassett, John S. "The Relation between the Virginia Planter and the London Merchant." American Historical Association Annual Report for 1901. Vol. 1.

Belding, Don. "End of an Era in Advertising." *Advertising Agency and Advertising and Selling* (July 1952).

Berman, Ronald. "Origins of the Art of Advertising." *The Journal of Aesthetic Education*, Vol. 17, No. 3 (Fall 1983).

Bliven, Bruce. "Can You Sell Goods to the 'Subconscious Mind'?" *Printers' Ink* (March 28, 1918).

Bok, Edward. "A Diabolical 'Patent-Medicine' Story." *The Ladies' Home Journal* (April 1905).

———. "The 'Patent-Medicine' Curse." *The Ladies' Home Journal* (May 1904).

———. "Why 'Patent Medicines' Are Dangerous." *The Ladies' Home Journal* (March 1905).

Bolton, Sarah K. "Little Biographies—How Success Is Won: IV. John Wanamaker." *Wide Awake* (January 1884).

Boston Chronicle, February 19, 1770.

The Boston News-Letter, April 17–24, May 1–8, May 15–22, June 5–11, August 21, 1704.

Brown, Thompson. "Hon. John Wanamaker. From Messenger-Boy to Merchant Prince. A Romance of Business." *Our Day*, Vol. 17, No. 113 (September 1897).

"Burning of Barnum's Museum." *New York Times*, March 3, 1868.

"Burning of Barnum's Museum." *New York Times*, March 4, 1868.

Bushman, Richard L., and Claudia L. Bushman. "The Early History of Cleanliness in America." *The Journal of American History*, Vol. 74, No. 4 (March 1988).

Cincinnati Gazette, June 19, 1838.

Clark, Francis E. "The Best-Known Name in America." *The Christian Endeavor World* (May 29, 1919).

"Colonel Springs Again." *Tide* (April 14, 1950).

"The Composition of Certain Secret Remedies." *The British Medical Journal* (July 1, 1911).

Coronet (August, November, December 1948; February, June, August, December 1949; February, April, June 1950).

Croll, P. C. "John Wanamaker: Merchant and Philanthropist." *The Pennsylvania-German* (January 1908).

Curti, Merle. "The Changing Concept of 'Human Nature' in the Literature of American Advertising." *Business History Review*, Vol. 41, No. 4 (Winter 1967).

Ellis, William T. "John Wanamaker Gave Sunday to Church and Sunday School." *North American* (December 30, 1922).

The General Magazine and Historical Chronicle, for All the British Plantations in America (January, May 1741).

Gleed, Charles S. "John Wanamaker." *The Cosmopolitan* (May 1902).

Gorgan, John B. "A Modern Business General." *The National Magazine: An Illustrated Monthly*, (October 1914).

Gray, Lewis C. "The Market Surplus Problems of Colonial Tobacco." *Agricultural History*, Vol. 2 (January 1928).

"Great Conflagration." *New York Tribune*, July 14, 1865.

"A Great Loss to Barnum." *New York Times*, November 21, 1887.

Harper's Weekly (January 5, 1895).

The Herald of Freedom, December 12, 1832.

Herzberg, Oscar. "The Evolution of Patent Medicine Advertising." *Printers' Ink* (December 25, 1895).

Hoffman, Ronald. "The Press in Mercantile Maryland: A Question of Utility." *Journalism Quarterly*, Vol. 46, No. 3 (Autumn 1969).

Holland, Donald R. "The Adman Nobody Knows: The Story of Volney Palmer, the Nation's First Agency Man." *Advertising Age* (April 23, 1973).

Hower, Ralph M. "Urban Retailing 100 Years Ago." *Bulletin of the Business Historical Society*, Vol. 12 (December 1938).

Hume, Ruth. "Selling the Swedish Nightingale: Jenny Lind and P. T. Barnum." *American Heritage* (October 1977).

"Indelible Mark on Advertising Left by Lasker, Agency Pioneer." *Advertising Age* (June 9, 1952).

The Independent, December 21, 1882.

James, Theodore, Jr. "World Went Mad When Mighty Jumbo Came to America." *Smithsonian* (May 1982).

Jones, Fred Mitchell. "Retail Stores in the United States 1800–1860." *Journal of Marketing*, Vol. 1, No. 2 (October 1936).

Klein, Maury. "John Wanamaker." *American History Illustrated*, Vol. 15, No. 8 (December 1980).

Kobre, Sidney. "The First American Newspaper: A Product of Environment." *Journalism Quarterly*, Vol. 17, No. 4 (December 1940).

————. "The Revolutionary Colonial Press—A Social Interpretation." *Journalism Quarterly*, Vol. 20, No. 3 (September 1943).

Kowall, Linda. "Original and Genuine, Unadulterated and Guaranteed!" *Pennsylvania Heritage*, Vol. 15, No. 1 (1989).

The Ladies' Home Journal (May 1896; December 1897; July 1910; May 1915; May 1925; January 1930).

Larrabee, C. B. "The Publisher Speaks: Bad Taste Leaves a Bad Taste." *Printers' Ink* (December 10, 1948).

Larson, Cedric. "Patent-Medicine Advertising and the Early American Press." *Journalism Quarterly*, Vol. 14, No. 4 (December 1937).

Lasker, Albert D. "The Personal Reminiscences of Albert Lasker." *American Heritage* (December 1954).

"The Late Fire." *New York Times*, July 15, 1865.

Lawson, Linda. "Advertisements Masquerading as News in Turn-of-the-Century American Periodicals." *American Journalism*, Vol. 5, No. 2 (1988).

Leach, William R. "Transformations in a Culture of Consumption: Women and Department Stores, 1890–1925." *The Journal of American History*, Vol. 71, No. 2 (September 1984).

Marburg, Theodore F. "Manufacturer's Drummer—1852." *Bulletin of the Business Historical Society*, Vol. 22 (June 1948).

M'Elroy's Philadelphia Directory (1842).

Montgomery, Charlotte. "The Woman's Viewpoint." *Tide*, September 10, 1948.

"Mrs. Lydia E. Pinkham's Vegetable Compound." *British Medical Journal* (July 1, 1911).

"The Museum Fire." *New York Times*, December 26, 1872.

New York Commercial Advertiser, February 29, 1850.

New York Daily Tribune, August 14, 1850.

"New York Fires." *New York Times*, December 25, 1872.

The New York Gazette, October 3–10, September 26–October 3, November 14–21, 1737.

The New York Herald, June 15, 1803.

New York Times, May 3, 1887.

The New York Weekly Journal, March 29, 1736.

Parker, Peter J. "The Philadelphia Printer: A Study of an Eighteenth-Century Businessman." *Business History Review*, Vol. 40, No. 1 (Spring 1966).

The Pennsylvania Gazette, September 25–October 2, 1729, August 14–21, 1735, July 1, 1736, June 23–30, 1737, January 18–25, 1738, 1739; November 13, 1740, June 17, 1742.

"People: How to Spend a Buck." *Newsweek* (October 26, 1959).

Pettengill, S. M. "Reminiscences of the Advertising Business." *Printers' Ink* (December 24, 1890).

Philadelphia Public Ledger, April 27, 1861.

"Playboy of the Textile World." *Fortune* (January 1950).

Plummer, Wilbur C. "Consumer Credit in Colonial Philadelphia." *Pennsylvania Magazine of History and Biography,* Vol. 67 (October 1942).

"The Recent Fires." *New York Times,* December 29, 1872.

Rice, Edwin Wilbur. "Mr. Wanamaker As I Knew Him." *The Sunday-School World* (March 1923).

Riis, Roger W. "A Critic Looks at Advertising." *Advertising Agency and Advertising and Selling* (October 1949).

Sangster, Margaret E. "John Wanamaker at Eighty: A Personal Interview." *The Christian Herald,* June 26, 1918.

The Saturday Evening Post (January 12, 1901, May 15, 1911).

Schiller, Zachary. "P & G Is Still Having a Devil of a Time." *Business Week* (September 11, 1995).

Schmidt, Louis B. "Internal Commerce and the Development of the National Economy before 1860." *Journal of Political Economy,* Vol. 47 (December 1939).

Schroeder, Fred E. H. "Feminine Hygiene, Fashion and the Emancipation of American Women." *American Studies,* Vol. 17 (1976).

Shaaber, Matthias A. "Forerunners of the Newspaper in America." *Journalism Quarterly,* Vol. 11, No. 3 (December 1934).

Shapiro, Stanley J. "Marketing in Massachusetts Bay Colony: 1629–1685." *Economics and Business Bulletin,* Temple University School of Business and Public Administration, Vol. 16 (December 1963).

Shaw, Steven J. "Colonial Newspaper Advertising: A Step toward Freedom of the Press." *Business History Review,* Vol. 33 (Autumn 1959).

Sherman, Sidney. "Advertising in the United States." *American Statistical Association Journal,* Vol. 7 (December 1900).

Smith, Roland B. "After Hours: Publicity Isn't Advertising." *Printers' Ink* (December 17, 1948).

Smythe, Ted Curtis. "The Advertisers' War to Verify Newspaper Circulation, 1870–1914." *American Journalism,* Vol. 3, No. 3 (1986).

"Springmaid." *Tide,* (July 16, 1948).

Sullivan, Mark. "Did Mr. Bok Tell the Truth?" *The Ladies' Home Journal* (January 1906).

——. "The Patent Medicine Conspiracy against the Freedom of the Press." *Collier's Weekly* (November 4, 1905).

The Tatler, September 12–14, 1710.

Taylor, James D. "Elliott White Springs—Maverick Ad Leader." *Journal of Advertising*, Vol. 11, No. 2 (1982).

"Textile Tempest." *Time* (July 26, 1948).

Thomas, Charles M. "The Publication of Newspapers during the American Revolution." *Journalism Quarterly*, Vol. 9, No. 4 (December 1932).

Thornley, Betty. "And the Merchant Princes Moved." *Vogue* (January 1923).

"Tide Leadership Survey." *Tide* (August 27, 1948).

Trytten, John M. "Sex in Advertising: The Easy Way Out!" *Sales Management* (May 28, 1973).

Venkatesan, M., and Jean Losco. "Women in Magazine Ads: 1959–71." *Journal of Advertising Research*, Vol. 15, No. 5 (October 1975).

Wallace, Wesley. "Property and Trade: Main Themes of Early North Carolina Newspaper Advertising." *North Carolina Historical Review*, Vol. 32 (October 1955).

Washburn, Robert Collyer. "Lydia Pinkham." *The American Mercury* (February 1931).

Westerfield, Roy B. "Early History of American Auctions: A Chapter in Commercial History." *Transactions of the Connecticut Academy of Arts and Sciences*, Vol. 23 (May 1920).

Wilder, Will. B. "Hypnotism in Advertising." *Fame* (September 1892).

Wooster, Harvey. "A Forgotten Factor in American Industrial History." *American Economic Review*, Vol. 16 (March 1926).

Index

About the Author

EDD APPLEGATE is a Professor in the School of Journalism at Middle Tennessee State University. His articles and reviews have been published in several academic journals, including *Journalism and Mass Communication Quarterly, Journalism and Mass Communication Educator, American Journalism, Journalism History*, and *Resources in Education*. He is the author of *Journalistic Advocates and Muckrakers: Three Centuries of Crusading Writers* (1997), *Literary Journalism: A Biographical Dictionary of Writers and Editors* (1996), and *Print and Broadcast Journalism: A Critical Examination* (1996) and the editor of *The Ad Men and Women: A Biographical Dictionary of Advertising* (1994), among other books.

ISBN 0-313-30364-9

90000>

EAN

9 780313 303647

HARDCOVER BAR CODE